MACHINE TRANSCRIPTION AND DICTATION

SIXTH EDITION

Mitsy Ballentine, M.Ed.
Greenville Technical College
South Carolina

SOUTH-WESTERN
CENGAGE Learning

Australia • Brazil • Japan • Korea • Mexico • Singapore • Spain • United Kingdom • United States

Machine Transcription and Dictation, Sixth Edition
Mitsy Ballentine

VP/Editorial Director: Jack W. Calhoun

Vice President/Editor-in-Chief: Karen Schmohe

Senior Acquisitions Editor: Jane Phelan

Sr. Development Editor: Dr. Inell Bolls

Consulting Editor: Peggy Shelton

Editorial Assistant: Conor Allen

Marketing Communications Manager: Tom Guenette

Senior Manufacturing Buyer: Charlene Taylor

Rights Acquisitions Account Manager, Text: PreMediaGlobal

Senior Art Director: Tippy McIntosh

Rights Acquisitions Account Manager, Text: PreMediaGlobal

Cover and Internal Designer: Craig Ramsdell, Ramsdell Design

Cover Image: © Igor Djurovic, Joshua Hodge Photography, claudiobaba: iStock © Pixotico, Andresr: Shutterstock; ©Juice Images, Getty Images

Compositor: PreMediaGlobal

For product information and technology assistance, contact us at
Cengage Learning Customer & Sales Support, 1-800-354-9706

For permission to use material from this text or product, submit all requests online at **cengage.com/permissions**
Further permissions questions can be emailed to
permissionrequest@cengage.com

Library of Congress Control Number: 2011925140

ISBN-13: 978-1-111-42545-6

ISBN-10: 1-111-42544-2

South-Western
5191 Natorp Boulevard
Mason, OH 45040
USA

Cengage Learning is a leading provider of customized learning solutions with office locations around the globe, including Singapore, the United Kingdom, Australia, Mexico, Brazil, and Japan. Locate your local office at: **international.cengage.com/region**

Cengage Learning products are represented in Canada by Nelson Education, Ltd.

For your course and learning solutions, visit **academic.cengage.com**

Purchase any of our products at your local college store or at our preferred online store **www.ichapters.com**
Microsoft is a registered trademark of Microsoft Corporation.

The names of all products mentioned herein are used for identification purposes only and may be trademarks or registered trademarks of their respective owners. Cengage disclaims any affiliation, association, connection with, sponsorship, or endorsement by such owners.

Printed in the United States of America
2 3 4 5 6 7 14 13 12

PREFACE

The Sixth Edition of *Machine Transcription and Dictation* provides students with the skills needed to transcribe a variety of documents and helps students strengthen their English skills. This text-workbook provides realistic documents from various fields of employment. This edition also includes a section on dictation and continuous speech recognition that gives students the opportunity to actually dictate and transcribe their own work.

This text-workbook is intended for students in vocational schools; adult education programs; career centers; office technology certificate, diploma, and degree programs at the post-secondary level; and secondary students enrolled in office careers courses.

Student Text-Workbook Organization

This edition is divided into four parts: basic machine transcription, intermediate machine transcription, advanced machine transcription—legal and medical, and dictation and continuous speech recognition. An instructor can assign one or all parts depending on whether this text-workbook is used as a complete course or as a supplement to another course.

Part 1, Basic Machine Transcription, gives experience in keying documents from various fields of employment. Punctuation is dictated within this part.

Part 2, Intermediate Machine Transcription, includes dictation from a variety of international dictators who will give very little punctuation as they dictate. Because we are a global society, there is an emphasis on using a variety of international dictators on the Transcription CD. This gives students an opportunity to develop their listening and transcribing skills while working with people who have different accents and dialects.

Part 3, Advanced Machine Transcription, concentrates on legal and medical dictation. Students are instructed to review all language skills previously learned because they will be tested on these skills; therefore, learning is reinforced and cumulative.

Part 4, Dictation and Continuous Speech Recognition, gives the student practice in dictating and learning about continuous speech recognition.

Key Features

Transcriptionist Profiles include personal profiles of actual transcriptionists.

Overview begins each chapter and includes specific objectives.

English Skills Review includes the following components:

- **Word Mastery Preview** includes business words that will be in the dictation given for each chapter.

- **Word Usage** presents groups of words that are commonly misused. The correct part of speech for each word is also given.

- **Spelling** sections contain a list of words that are commonly misspelled.

- **Language Skills** provide a review of basic grammar, punctuation, capitalization, figure/number, and word division rules.
- **Proofreading Tips** provide quick and easy methods for improving proofreading skills.

English Skills Exercises allow students to apply what they learned in the English Skills Review section.

Composition exercises are provided to allow students to compose paragraphs utilizing the vocabulary and English skills learned.

Research exercises give students the opportunity to use the library and Internet to learn more about careers by seeking answers to questions.

Transcription Preview includes specific information that will help students transcribe documents in the correct format.

Transcription Exercises provide the directions students need to transcribe the dictation from the Transcription CD.

Chapter Checkpoints are included to allow students to assess whether they have met the overall objectives of each chapter.

A **Reference Manual** includes a summary of all proofreading guidelines, language skills, document formatting, and other helpful resource information.

New to This Edition

In addition to retaining features from the previous edition, the following features have been added or modified for the new Sixth Edition:

1. Each part features a transcriptionist profile. Transcriptionist interviews provide real-world knowledge and advice about transcriptionist careers.

2. Additional transcription exercises are included. Each chapter has at least one more document added. Part 3, which includes legal and medical dictation, has two documents added to each chapter.

3. The English Skills Review has been expanded. In each chapter, this section now includes the following:
   - Word Mastery Preview
   - Word Usage
   - Spelling
   - Language Skills
   - Proofreading Tips

4. The English Skills Exercises have been expanded to include twice as many exercises as in previous editions.

5. The Composition and Research segments have been updated.

6. Transcription Previews are new to this edition. They help the student learn how to format documents that will be dictated in Word 2007 format.

7. The Evaluation Forms have been moved out of the text-workbook and are now included on the Transcription CD for easy access by students. These forms also are included on the IRCD. Two Evaluation Forms are available—one for use with the chapters and one for use with Part 4. These forms can be used by the students as a cover sheet for submitting work to the instructor. They can be used by the instructor to give feedback to students.

8. Additional student learning reinforcement is provided at the following website: www.cengage.com/officetech/ballentine

ACKNOWLEDGMENTS

The author would like to thank all those who contributed support or suggestions for this edition of the text-workbook, particularly the reviewers listed below. The author would like to dedicate this text-workbook to Dennis, Nathan, Karen, Sarah, J.C., and Emma.

REVIEWERS

Patricia A. Cameron
Instructor, Medical Department
Bryant & Stratton College
Liverpool, New York

Janeen E. Duer
Business and Keyboarding Instructor
Ridley-Lowell Business and Technical Institute
New London, Connecticut

Deborah A. Franklin
Office Technology Instructor
Bryant & Stratton College
Orchard Park, New York

Heather Hughes, BA, NCMA
Medical Assisting Program Lead
Sanford Brown Institute
Cranston, Rhode Island

Laura Soldani, MAE, CPC
Business Instructor
Bryant & Stratton College
Albany, New York

TABLE OF CONTENTS

PART 1
Basic Machine Transcription

TRANSCRIPTIONIST PROFILE

Kathryn Drury, Plainfield, VT
Self-Employed, Freelance Transcriptionist

Why did you decide to do this type of work?

"I fell into it. When I was about 22, I got a summer job in a business services office, and one of the tasks was to transcribe some material. I was introduced to the foot pedal with backspace, and all I had to do was type the conversation. I didn't really decide to do it. I was asked to do it."

Who inspired you to consider working in transcription?

"I inspired myself. I really loved the transcription part of my office job. I'm an incredibly fast typist, and I loved hearing people tell stories. Because I'm good at transcribing, I found it low pressure and even relaxing."

Where did you learn how to transcribe?

"I was taught to transcribe on the job. No one else wanted to do it, so I did it. And the more I did it, the faster and better I became."

Keep apprised of current events so you can understand rapid references. Familiarize yourself thoroughly with Microsoft Word and with various audio formats (MP3, WAV, CDs, and so forth).

When did you first begin transcribing?

"When I was actually job hunting, I saw an ad for 'transcribers.' I went to take a test and was hired on the spot. I transcribed for this company for several years, but it was for the financial world and was pretty boring—CEOs and money managers talking about the market. My interests are writing and film, so I thought it would be more interesting to transcribe for documentary filmmakers and journalists. I started my own freelance business doing that, and I've been doing it for close to 15 years now!"

How did you educationally prepare for your current position?

"I am an avid reader and have always had a strong feeling for language. I keep up with current events. I've also been a listener all my life, so it is easy for me to catch onto what people are talking about, even if they are from a world I have never seen."

What do you enjoy the most and the least about transcribing?

"What I enjoy most about transcribing is hearing people's stories and being exposed to new worlds, new ways of talking, and new ways of saying things. I enjoy the challenge of keying an excellent transcript and the appreciation I get from the people who have hired me. These transcripts are so helpful to their work. I take the time to Google all terminology that I'm not familiar with so my transcripts are clean and well informed. I also enjoy having my own schedule. I am a single mother with three kids. I transcribe while the kids are at school, and if I'm on a deadline, I transcribe when they are in bed. I can work and also participate in my kid's lives. Also, I love working at home because there is no commute, and I can wear blue jeans every day. The downside is that it's not social. I do all my work via e-mail."

What advice would you give a student regarding transcription?

"I recently transcribed for a historian of Chinese Art, which I knew nothing about. When you don't know anything about the subject matter, do a little research first to become familiar with basic terminology. In addition, keep apprised of current events so you can understand rapid references. Familiarize yourself thoroughly with Microsoft Word and with various audio formats (MP3, WAV, CDs, and so forth)."

©Andresr/Shutterstock.com

LEARNING OBJECTIVES

After completing all the learning activities in this chapter, you will be able to:

- Define, spell, and use the Word Mastery terms.

- Use commonly misused words appropriately.

- Use correct spelling for commonly misspelled words.

- Recognize and correct incomplete sentences and apply the subject-verb agreement rules presented in this chapter.

- Apply the rules for capitalization presented in this chapter.

- Apply proofreading and transcription skills.

- Transcribe documents in unbound report format.

Chapter 1
MACHINE TRANSCRIPTION

Office professionals who have excellent office skills, good interpersonal skills, superior work ethics, and professional appearance and attitudes are always in great demand. The skills you will learn in this course will be extremely beneficial to you no matter what position or field you may pursue. In addition to operating the equipment and transcribing documents, you will increase your listening skills, your English skills, and proofreading skills. You will also have the opportunity to transcribe documents used in many different fields of employment and dictated by a variety of people with different accents and dialects.

ENGLISH SKILLS REVIEW

 Word Mastery Preview

Directions: Review the list of Word Mastery terms that will be used in the documents you will be transcribing. Learn the definition of each word and how to spell it correctly.

transcribe
Definition: to make a written or typed copy of dictated material
Example: Stephanie's boss asked her to transcribe his speech.

dictation
Definition: words that are dictated and recorded by a person
Example: When he had taken the dictation from his employer, he immediately began to transcribe the material.

fluency
Definition: ability to flow smoothly
Example: His fluency in using the French language impressed all of us.

rewind
Definition: to turn backwards
Example: You will need to rewind the dictation to hear the beginning.

fast-forward
Definition: to move ahead
Example: If you fast-forward, you can get to the end of the dictation quickly.

valuable
Definition: having considerable worth
Example: Leon considered his knowledge of English skills to be extremely valuable.

machine transcriptionist
Definition: a person who transcribes dictation using a dictation/transcription unit
Example: Robert hoped to obtain a job as a medical machine transcriptionist when he completed his training.

formatting
Definition: putting information into a completed or final form
Example: When she had decided on the proper formatting for the letter, she began to key the document.

reference
Definition: compiled information used as a source
Example: What reference material did you use for your report?

rekeying
Definition: to type again
Example: Rekeying was necessary because of the numerous errors.

| transcription equipment | *Definition:* | equipment used to listen to material that has been recorded |
| | *Example:* | Our transcription equipment was broken so we ordered another unit. |

| centralized | *Definition:* | in one location |
| | *Example:* | The filing system was centralized. |

| microcassettes | *Definition:* | small holders of magnetic tape that are used to record dictation; smaller than minicassettes |
| | *Example:* | People use microcassettes to record dictation on the portable units. |

| minicassettes | *Definition:* | small holders of magnetic tape that are used to record dictation |
| | *Example:* | Minicassettes are used with some desktop units. |

| microphone | *Definition:* | a device used by a speaker to record dictation |
| | *Example:* | Please speak directly into the microphone. |

| originators | *Definition:* | people who create documents |
| | *Example:* | You may need to check with the originators to find out if the documents need to be transcribed today. |

| endless loop | *Definition:* | nonremovable media used to record dictation on a central system; a continuous loop where new dictation records on top of the old dictation |
| | *Example:* | The endless loop on our central dictation system had to be replaced after so many years of use. |

B Word Usage

Directions: Learn to spell and define these confusing words, which may occur within the documents you will be transcribing.

| **a lot** | (adverb) many; much |
| **alot** | not a word; do not use |

| **accept** | (verb) to receive |
| **except** | (verb or preposition) to exclude; with the exclusion of |

| **few** | (noun or adjective) a smaller amount (can be counted) |
| **less** | (noun or adjective) a smaller amount or degree (cannot be counted) |

good	(adjective) skillful; admirable; having the right qualities
well	(adverb) properly; with skill; a person's well-being and health

in	(preposition) inside a location
into	(preposition) entering something

passed	(verb) moved beyond; to go pass
past	(noun or adjective) opposite of future; former

to	(preposition) toward
too	(adverb) also
two	(noun) the number 2

 ## Spelling

Directions: Learn to spell these common words.

across	describe	lesson
beneficial	develop	neither
calendar	either	omission
career	equipment	perform
decide	finally	pertaining

 ## Language Skills

Directions: Enhance your language skills by reviewing basic grammar, punctuation, capitalization, number/figure style, abbreviation style, and word division rules. Study the rules and examples below. All language skills rules also appear in the reference manual at the back of your text-workbook.

Rule: A sentence is a complete thought and includes a subject and a verb. The **subject** (single underscore in the examples) is a noun or pronoun. A **noun** is a person, place, or thing. A **pronoun** takes the place of a noun. The word *you* can be an understood subject, which means it is not stated but implied. The **verb** (double underscore in the examples) expresses action or a state of being.

Examples:
- Go to the store. (The subject *you* is implied.)
- Mary will give me the information.

Rule: Do not use two sentences as one sentence. This produces a run-on sentence. Two sentences must be separated either by a period or a semicolon or a comma with a conjunction.

Examples:
- Rubeanna can handle the job. Joseph will not be able to perform his duties.
- Many people would like to own their own businesses; Gabriel has owned his own business for three years.

- Keyboarding skills are essential for today's office employee, and the knowledge of various software application packages is desired.

Rule: A group of words must express a complete thought to be a complete sentence. If the thought is not complete even though it includes a subject and verb, it is a fragment or a dependent clause.

Examples:
- If we have the answers to the problem (Fragment or dependent clause)

- If we have the answers to the problem, we can proceed with the experiment. (Complete sentence)

Rule: The subject and verb must agree in person and number. A singular subject must have a singular verb; a plural subject must have a plural verb. A clue that will help you in determining singular/plural subjects and singular/plural verbs is that most singular subjects (document, principal, boy, girl, presentation, and so forth) do not end in the letter *s*; most singular verbs do end in the letter *s* (is, has, was, talks, looks, seems, and so forth). Most plural subjects end in the letter *s* (documents, principals, boys, girls, presentations, and so forth); most plural verbs do not end in the letters *s* (are, have, were, talk, look, seem, and so forth).

Sometimes, subjects are joined by conjunctions. If the conjunction is the word *and,* the subject is plural and requires a plural verb. If the conjunction is the word *or,* use the verb that agrees with the subject closest to the verb. When correlative conjunctions (neither/nor, either/or, both/and) are used with subjects, use the verb that agrees with the subject closest to the verb. Subjects of sentences are not found within a prepositional phrase (a group of words that begins with a preposition).

Examples:
- The <u>document</u> <u>was</u> not <u>received</u>. (*Document* is a singular subject; *was received* is a singular verb.)

- The <u>documents</u> <u>were received</u>. (The word *documents* is a plural subject; *were received* is a plural verb.)

- <u>Mary</u> and <u>Jane</u> <u>were</u> absent. (*Mary* and *Jane* are plural subjects; *were* is the plural verb.)

- The <u>boys</u> or their <u>principal</u> <u>is going</u> to lead the entire school into the auditorium. (Because the word *or* is joining two subjects and *principal* is singular and closest to the verb, the singular verb *is going* is used.)

- Neither the <u>principal</u> nor the <u>boys</u> <u>are going</u> to lead the entire school into the auditorium. (Because *neither/nor* is used, the plural verb *are going* is used since the subject *boys* is plural and closest to the verb.)

- Either the <u>girls</u> or the <u>teacher</u> <u>is going</u> to lead the entire school into the auditorium. (Because *either/or* is used, the singular verb *is going* is used since the subject *teacher* is singular and closest to the verb.)

- The <u>presentation</u> of the various projects <u>was</u> not on the agenda. (Although the word *projects* is plural and closest to the verb, it is part of a prepositional phrase and cannot be the subject. The subject is *presentation* and is singular; therefore, the singular verb *was* is used.)

Rule: Capitalize the first word of a sentence.

Examples:
- May we go get the transcribed documents for you.
- Yes, you may pick up the finished transcription.

Proofreading
Tips

- When proofreading any document, assume there are errors and look for them as though you were the instructor grading your assignment.

- Do not rely on spelling and grammar features in software programs to correct all errors. Certain types of errors are not recognized by the software.

- Mark corrections using proofreaders' marks, which are shown in the reference manual at the back of this text-workbook.

ENGLISH SKILLS EXERCISES

A Word Mastery

Directions: Apply what you learned in the English Skills Review. Choose the correct word in the following sentences from those found in the Word Mastery Preview.

1. You will need to listen to the _____ on the CD before you can transcribe the material.

2. If you _____, you will be able to listen to the information again.

3. The office manager gave the dictation to the _____ and asked her to have the material keyed as soon as possible.

4. When you are unsure of the correct document _____, you need to review the various styles in a reference manual.

5. Emma's instructor asked her to transcribe the _____ on the CD.

6. Although Orfa had moved from Colombia to America only a year ago, her _____ in English was impressive.

7. A good transcriptionist will keep many _____ books nearby when transcribing to check spelling, format style, and so forth.

Word Mastery (continued)

8. Karen and Nathan found having good English and grammar skills was essential when they began to _____ the dictation from their employers.

9. If you key the document correctly the first time, _____ will not be necessary.

10. Although _____ and _____ have been used to hold recorded dictation in the past, transcriptionists now find dictation is stored on other forms of media.

B Word Usage

Directions: Choose the correct word in each of the following sentences.

1. Do not (except, accept) the decision until everyone has given his or her input.
2. We will have to (except, accept) the instructor's grade on our project.
3. We need (to, too, two) get the supplies ordered by next week.
4. The children want ice cream (to, too, two).
5. Joseph did not do (good, well) on his exam.
6. Mary and Joan did not sing (good, well) during the recital.
7. I have (a lot, alot) of work to do before I can submit my proposal.
8. We went (in, into) the classroom and found (few, less) students there.
9. (In, Into) the middle of the night, I heard my cat making a noise.
10. My teacher (past, passed) me in the hallway.

C Spelling

Directions: Choose the correct spelling in each of the following sentences.

1. The (calendar, calander) was (finally, finaly) on her boss's desk.
2. Do you think you can (describe, discribe) the type of (career, carer) you want?
3. There were many different types of (equippment, equipment) found in the basement.
4. (Niether, Neither) the reporter nor her supervisor saw the error before it was printed.
5. What (ommission, omission) do you think you made in your (lesson, lessen)?
6. Studying can be (benificial, beneficial) for everyone.
7. Don't go (across, accross) the line that is on the floor.
8. Do you think the information (pertaining, purtaining) to the situation was given?
9. We need to (purform, perform) many tasks before our meeting.
10. (Develop, Develope) the project further before we (deside, decide) to present it.

D Language Skills

Directions: Use proofreaders' marks to make corrections in the following sentences. Refer to the proofreaders' marks in the reference manual at the back of this text-workbook. Write "Correct" by the sentence if no corrections are needed.

1. I will be glad to go to the party.

2. Willis is not going to present the information at the meeting, Rachel will be the one to give the presentation.

3. Stop!

4. Because I want to do well in this course.

5. A table, a chair, and a desk is all the pieces of furniture we will need for our office.

6. we need to have enough material for the presentation we want to be prepared.

7. The cost of the repairs are too high.

8. Let's begin the meeting on time.

9. If we don't understand the reason.

10. The reason for the delays were not explained.

E Composition

1. Compose and key a paragraph applying the word mastery, word usage, spelling, and language skills you have studied.
2. Compose and key a second paragraph that explains what it means to express a complete thought.
3. Compose and key a third paragraph that explains why the spell-check feature might not find errors keyed in a document. Submit all three paragraphs to your instructor.

F Research

1. Conduct research using the Internet, newspaper, and library or talk with individuals who are actually employed in the machine transcription field to obtain information about the topics listed below. When searching online, go to the U.S. Bureau of Labor Statistics website at **www.bls.gov** and click on the **Publications** tab. Then click on the ***Occupational Outlook Handbook*** and **Index** links. Click on the first letter of the name of the field. (Example: Click on the letter *T* and scroll down the screen to find information on *transcription.*) You can also do an online search of the name of the field/industry followed by the words *career* or *training*. (Example: *transcription career* or *transcription training*)

   • What are the employment opportunities for office workers in machine transcription?

   • What are the advantages and/or disadvantages of using machine transcription equipment?

   • What skills or characteristics are necessary for becoming an expert transcriptionist?

   • What are the job titles or positions in the transcription field?

Research (*continued*)

- What are the salary ranges for positions in this field?

- What additional information did you learn during this research?

2. Compose a document by keying paragraphs that address the questions above. Add a meaningful title. Include your name and the date. Proofread, edit, and revise the paragraphs to correct all grammar and spelling errors. Print the document. Proofread it again and make any final changes before submitting it to your instructor.

TRANSCRIPTION PREVIEW

The Transcription Preview section of each chapter includes specific information that will help you transcribe the documents in correct format or provides other special instructions for getting started. In Chapter 1, you will review setting up your Transcription CD and keying a document in unbound report format.

Transcription CD

You will use the Transcription CD located in the back of your text-workbook to transcribe the documents in each lesson. Install the Transcription CD by inserting it into your CD-ROM drive. The program will automatically launch. The Transcription CD includes the following links:

Using Your Machine Transcription CD Select this link to print directions for using the CD. It includes instructions for installing either Express Scribe or Windows Media Player software, which is to be used to transcribe the documents.

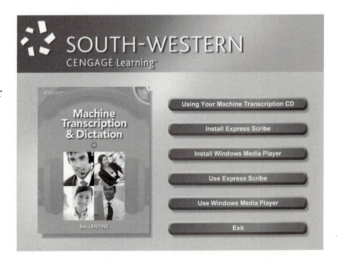

Install Express Scribe
Install Windows Media Player Use either of these links to install the software of your choice. Listen to the audio presentation that explains how to use the software. The software also includes a user's guide or help feature. Express Scribe is recommended and provided free of charge by NCH Software. Windows Media Player may already be installed on your computer as part of the Windows installation process.

Use Express Scribe
Use Windows Media Player Select either of these buttons when you're ready to begin transcribing. A dialog box will display the chapters and documents that are available. Click the "Launch Lesson" button to begin.

Exit Select this button to quit.

Transcription Methods

After you have installed either the Express Scribe or Windows Media Player software, you will be ready to transcribe documents. Depending on the system you are using, you may use a foot pedal, mouse, or function keys to start, stop, rewind, and fast-forward your dictation. Your instructor will tell you which method to use. Directions for using each method are provided below.

Using Express Scribe (foot pedal or keystroke control method):

1. Plug your headset and foot pedal (if you are not going to use the keystroke method) into the computer using the manufacturer's recommended settings.

2. Insert the Transcription CD and select "Use Express Scribe" from the main menu.

3. Select the chapter and the document you wish to open and click the "Launch Lesson" button. The program will automatically open Word and Express Scribe. A template file for the document will also open.

4. If you are using a foot pedal, you will use it to stop, play, rewind, and fast-forward the dictation.

5. If you are using keystrokes (function keys) to operate the dictation playback, here is a listing of some of the hot keys you will want to use to control the dictation:

   F4 Stops the dictation

   F9 Plays the dictation

   F7 Rewinds the dictation

   F8 Fast-forwards the dictation

Using Windows Media Player (mouse control method):

1. Plug your headset into the computer using the manufacturer's recommended settings.

2. Insert the Transcription CD and select "Use Windows Media Player" from the main menu.

3. Select the chapter and the document you wish to open, and click on the "Launch Lesson" button. Word will launch, and a template file for the document will open. The Media Player console will appear on top of it.

4. Use your mouse to increase and decrease volume, start and stop, fast-forward to the end, or rewind to the beginning. The slider bar may be used to fast-forward and rewind within the dictation lesson.

Transcription Procedures

As you begin transcribing documents, you should follow the procedures described below.

Standard Transcription Procedures

Listen to an ear full, stop the dictation, and key the document.

Repeat the procedure of listening, stopping the dictation if necessary, and transcribing until you have keyed the completed document.

Stop and replay the dictation whenever you need to listen to a group of words again.

Fast-forward whenever you need to proceed more quickly through the recording.

Save each document using a distinctive file name. For example, for Document 1, use the title of the report and the date as the file name.
Example: Transcription Guidelines 05_11_20XX

Capitalization in Dictation:

When a word should be capitalized, the dictator will say, "Capital."
Example: I need to see (Capital) John today.

When each major word in a group of related words should be capitalized, the dictator will say, "Caps."
Example: I will attend the meeting at the (Caps) American Institute of Technology.

When entire words should appear in all capital letters, the dictator will say, "All Caps."
Example: Please read the textbook I gave you entitled (All Caps) PROOFREADING MADE EASY.

Unbound Report Format

All the documents in this chapter will be keyed in an unbound report format. Review the proper format for unbound reports described below and on the next page.

Margins: Use default 1" top, side, and bottom margins.

Font Size: Use the default 11-point Calibri font.

Spacing: Use the default 1.15 line spacing for the body of the report.

Title:

- Tap ENTER three times to position the title at about 2".
- Capitalize the first letter of all main words.
- Select the title and apply the Title style, which is 26-point Cambria font, dark blue, left aligned, with a bottom border. (If the title is long, click Shrink Font from the Fonts group and reduce the font size so that the title appears on one line.)
- Tap ENTER once after the title.

Side Heading (if a side heading is dictated):

- Key side heading at the left margin.
- Capitalize the first letter of all main words.
- Apply Heading 1 style, which is 14-point Cambria font.
- Tap ENTER once after the heading.

2" (Tap ENTER three times.)

Title → # Electronic Mail Guidelines Title style

Electronic mail, a widely used communication channel in the business environment, clearly has three major advantages—time effectiveness, distance effectiveness, and cost effectiveness. To reap full benefit from this common and convenient communication medium, follow the basic guidelines regarding the creation and use of e-mail when used for business purposes.

Side heading → ## Message Content Heading 1 style

Although perceived as informal documents, e-mail messages are business records. Therefore, follow these effective communication guidelines.

1"

Bulleted list →

- Write clear, concise sentences, avoiding clichés, slang, redundancies, and wordiness.
- Avoid emoticons and text message jargon or acronyms.
- Break the message into logical paragraphs, sequencing in an appropriate order. White space is important in e-mail messages as well as printed documents, so be sure to add extra space between paragraphs.
- Limit e-mail messages to one idea per message, and preferably limit to one screen.
- Always include a subject line that clearly defines the e-mail message.
- Consider carefully the recipients of the e-mail; do not waste your colleagues' valuable time by sending or copying unnecessary e-mails.
- Spell-check e-mail messages carefully; verify punctuation and content accuracy.
- Check the tone of the message carefully. If angry, wait at least one hour before clicking the Send button. Review the message, modify if needed, and then send the message.

1"

Preferences

Although e-mail is a common means of communication, other methods include face-to-face communication, telephone, voice mail, and instant messaging. It is important to realize that each person has preferred methods of communication, and the method will vary depending upon the message content. To accomplish tasks more effectively, be aware of individuals' preferred channels of communication and use those channels if appropriate for the business purpose.

Remember that effective communication is essential to be successful in today's business world. Apply these important guidelines as you prepare e-mail messages.

Source: VanHuss, Forde, and Woo, *Keyboarding & Word Processing Essentials*, 18e, South-Western Cengage Learning, 2010.

1. Insert the Transcription CD into your CD-ROM drive. Select either "Use Express Scribe" or "Use Windows Media Player." Review the directions on page 13 for using the software.

2. Transcribe the Word Mastery terms from the Transcription CD.

3. Following the Standard Transcription Procedures described on page 14, transcribe the five documents from the Transcription CD in unbound report format. When you launch each document, a template file will open. In Chapter 1, this will be a plain sheet of paper.

4. Save the file for each document using a distinctive file name.

5. Spell-check, proofread, and submit all five documents to your instructor for approval.

CHAPTER CHECKPOINTS

Place a check mark beside the objectives you can meet after completing this chapter.

_____ I can define, spell, and use the Word Mastery terms in this chapter.

_____ I can use the commonly misused terms from the Word Usage section in this chapter.

_____ I can spell correctly the words in the Spelling section in this chapter.

_____ I can recognize and correct incomplete sentences and use the proper subject-verb agreement rules presented in the Language Skills section in this chapter.

_____ I can apply the rules for capitalization presented in the Language Skills section in this chapter.

_____ I can transcribe documents in unbound report format and proofread carefully.

Evaluation Form

Access the Evaluation Form from your Transcription CD. Complete it and submit it with your work. You may choose to either print the form and complete it or complete the form electronically.

©rale/Shutterstock.com

Chapter 2
ADVERTISING, JOURNALISM, AND PUBLISHING

The fields of advertising, journalism, and publishing offer exciting careers, especially if you enjoy English and writing. Usually a college education with a major in one of these fields is required for entering into these occupations.

ENGLISH SKILLS REVIEW

A Word Mastery Preview

Directions: Review the list of Word Mastery terms that will be used in the documents you will be transcribing. Learn the definition for each word and how to spell it correctly.

proposal	*Definition:*	a plan or an offer to be accepted or rejected
	Example:	You have submitted a proposal for this project to the correct individual.
autobiography	*Definition:*	an account of a person's life written by her/himself
	Example:	Andre Agassi's autobiography was most unusual.
royalties	*Definition:*	compensation based on a portion of the proceeds
	Example:	The author did not receive the royalties she had expected.
editor	*Definition:*	a person who has managerial and decision-making responsibilities at a publishing, newspaper, or magazine firm
	Example:	When the editor approves this text, we can begin printing it.
accommodate	*Definition:*	to provide or supply
	Example:	If we can accommodate your needs in any way, please let us know.
commercial	*Definition:*	an announcement advertising or promoting a product
	Example:	The commercial for our newest product did not draw as much interest as we had hoped.
manuscript	*Definition:*	an author's draft of her/his work
	Example:	Every manuscript received by our office is reviewed.
fiction	*Definition:*	a piece of work that is not based on true events
	Example:	Many works of fiction often seem true to life.
expertise	*Definition:*	skill or knowledge
	Example:	Your expertise in English provided the information we needed.
campaign	*Definition:*	a systematic course of action or activities
	Example:	The campaign will start this fall.

B Word Usage

Directions: Learn to spell and define these confusing **words, which** may occur within the documents you will be transcribing.

affect	(verb) to influence
effect	(noun or verb) outcome or result; to bring about
both	(adjective or pronoun) two items or people considered collectively
each	(adjective or pronoun) any number of items or people considered separately
can	(verb) able to do something
may	(verb) possibility or used in seeking permission
cite	(verb) to quote
site	(noun) location
sight	(noun or verb) something that is seen; the ability to see; to see
every day	(noun) each day
everyday	(adjective) routine; common
stationary	(adjective) not moving
stationery	(noun) paper used for writing correspondence
who's	(pronoun) the contraction for *who is*
whose	(pronoun) possessive form of *who*

C Spelling

Directions: Learn to spell these common words.

advertisement	**library**	**proper**
chapters	**miscellaneous**	**punctuation**
convenience	**original**	**speech**
extraordinary	**plagiarize**	**spelling**
imitation	**playwright**	**writing**

D Language Skills

Directions: Enhance your language skills by reviewing basic grammar, punctuation, capitalization, number/figure style, abbreviation style, and word division rules. Study the rules and examples below.

Rule: Use a comma to set off a dependent clause at the beginning of a sentence from the independent clause. (A dependent clause is a group of words that have a subject and verb but cannot stand alone as a complete sentence. An independent clause is a group of words that have a subject and verb and can stand alone as a complete sentence.)

Examples:
- If the package doesn't come this morning, call me.
- When you see the editor, let him know I need to discuss some projects with him.

Rule: Use a comma or commas to set off a word or words that rename words they follow.

Examples:
- My best friend, Maria Sieradzki, moved away several weeks ago.
- Sorrento's, my favorite restaurant, is located off Main Street.

Rule: Use a comma to set off parenthetical words or phrases that are not needed in the sentence.

Examples:
- Linda Guissentanner, for example, has already completed her report.
- We will, of course, be glad to attend the fundraising event.

Rule: Capitalize names of people.

Examples:
- Our author's name is John Smith.
- Is your editor's name Janet Morton or Janette Morton?

Rule: Capitalize courtesy titles (Mr., Mrs., Miss, Ms.) before names.

Examples:
- Please give your manuscript to Ms. Inell Phelan.
- Did Mr. Brandt receive the proposal from our client?

Rule: Capitalize the brand names of products but not the product itself.

Examples:
- Why don't you see if he wants us to buy the Microsoft keyboard?
- My company prefers to use Canon digital cameras.

Rule: Capitalize only the first letter of the important words in headings and titles. Conjunctions, articles, and prepositions are not normally capitalized unless they are the first word of the heading or title. Titles of books should be italicized, underlined, or keyed in all capital letters.

Examples:
- *Alice in Wonderland* was a success for Lewis Carroll.
- <u>Alice in Wonderland</u> was a success for Lewis Carroll.
- ALICE IN WONDERLAND was a success for Lewis Carroll.

ENGLISH SKILLS EXERCISES

A Word Mastery

Directions: Apply what you learned in the English Skills Review. Choose the correct word in the following sentences from those found in the Word Mastery Preview.

1. We feel the _____ for the project did not address all the points that need to be covered before it can be approved.

2. Although we can _____ your request for the information, we will not be able to send it to you by the date you desire.

3. An individual may write his or her own _____, but most people prefer that someone else write about their life.

4. Our _____ will have to approve all the material before it is released.

5. Because of his _____ in that field, we were able to complete the project on time.

6. The author hoped to receive 10 percent in _____ for his work.

7. When you see a(n) _____ on television, remember that its purpose is to entice you to buy the product being advertised.

8. The political _____ was involving more work than anticipated.

9. If you like to read material not based on true facts, then you would want to read _____ not non-fiction books.

10. The reviewers were impressed with the author's first-draft _____ for his book.

B Word Usage

Directions: Choose the correct word in each of the following sentences.

1. Please hand me the company (stationary, stationery) from the desk drawer so I can use it to print the letters I keyed.

2. (Who's, Whose) job is being terminated next week?

3. Crystal Rosti worked on her manuscript (everyday, every day).

4. Although she was young, she hoped she would be able to (affect, effect) her peers.

5. (Whose, Who's) the person we are to contact regarding the project?

6. (Can, May) I have the information you prepared yesterday?

7. Since you know Italian better than I do, you (may, can) be the interpreter while we are on vacation.

8. (Both, Each) of you will work on the next book together.

9. Let's (cite, site, sight) that comment in the chapter at the end of the author's book.

10. What (cite, site, sight) do you want to use to tape the commercial for our product?

C Spelling

Directions: Choose the correct spelling in each of the following sentences.

1. After we finished reading the first few (chapters, chaptures), we knew the book would be succesful.

2. There were many (miscellaneous, miscellanious) details that had to be completed before the manuscript was ready.

3. When you (plagiarize, plagerize), you are using someone else's work as your own.

4. Wasn't the editor's (speech, speach) at the award's banquet eloquent?

5. Arthur Miller was a famous (playwright, playwrite, playright).

6. The (convenience, convenence) of having a (library, libary) so close to my home is wonderful.

7. Check your (punctuation, punctuiation) and (spelling, sppelling) when you proofread your (writting, writing).

8. After you have seen the (original, origenal) production, you won't desire to see the others.

9. (Extraordinery, Extraordinary) measures were taken to be sure the movie was similar to the book.

10. Perhaps this (emitation, imitation) will make you think you have the real item.

D Language Skills

Directions: Use proofreaders' marks to make corrections in the following sentences. Write "Correct" by the sentence if no corrections are needed.

1. If we receive the information in time we can complete our project.

2. My English teacher mr. Jackson has taught at our school for over 32 years.

3. We can of course expect to have a large group attend the wedding.

4. I did not enjoy reading the book entitled <u>up on a mountain</u>.

5. <u>Gone with the wind</u> was a book before it became a movie.

6. John anderson loves to eat Wendy's Hamburgers.

7. Jacob Nanney our editor will have to approve the material.

8. When we receive the material, we will be able to process your order.

9. As we review the manuscript we can determine what changes need to be made.

10. Because several people would be attending the meeting Ellen used the kodak photocopier to make copies of her report for everyone.

E Composition

1. Compose and key a paragraph applying the word mastery, word usage, spelling, and language skills you have studied.

2. Compose and key a second paragraph that explains the difference between an autobiography and a work of fiction.

3. Compose and key a third paragraph that describes the skills and knowledge that might help you prepare a manuscript for publication. Submit all three paragraphs to your instructor.

F Research

1. Conduct research using the Internet, newspaper, and library or talk with individuals who are actually employed in the advertising, journalism, and publishing fields to obtain information about the topics listed below. When searching online, go to the U.S. Bureau of Labor Statistics website at **www.bls.gov** and click on the **Publications** tab. Then click on the ***Occupational Outlook Handbook*** and **Index** links. Click on the first letter of the name of the field. (Example: Click on the letter *A* and scroll down the screen to find information on *advertising*.) You can also do an online search of the name of the field/industry followed by the words *career* or *training*. (Example: *advertising career* or *advertising training*)

   • What are the employment opportunities for office workers in the advertising, journalism, or publishing fields?

   • What are the advantages and/or disadvantages of employment in these fields?

Research (*continued*)

- What skills or characteristics are necessary for someone who wants to work in these fields?
- What are the job titles or positions in these fields?
- What are the salary ranges for positions in these fields?
- What additional information did you learn during this research?

2. Compose a document by keying paragraphs that address the questions above. Add a meaningful title. Include your name and the date. Proofread, edit, and revise the paragraphs to correct all grammar and spelling errors. Print the document. Proofread it again and make any final changes before submitting it to your instructor.

TRANSCRIPTION PREVIEW

The documents in this chapter will be keyed in block letter style with open punctuation. Review the proper format described below and on the next page.

Block Letter Style

Page Settings:

- Use default 1" top, side, and bottom margins.
- Use the default 11-point Calibri font and 1.15 line spacing.
- Begin all lines at the left margin.

Date Line: Position the current date at about 2" (tap ENTER three times). Be sure to begin at least 0.5" below the letterhead.

Letter Address: Begin the letter address two lines below the date (tap ENTER twice). Be sure to remove the extra space between the lines in the letter address.

Salutation: Key the salutation one line below the letter address (tap ENTER once).

Body: Begin the body one line below the salutation. Tap ENTER once between paragraphs.

Complimentary Closing: Position the complimentary closing one line below the body (tap ENTER once).

Writer's Name and Title: Begin the writer's name and title two lines below the complimentary closing (tap ENTER twice).

Reference Initials: Key the reference initials in lowercase one line below the the writer's name/title (tap ENTER once).

Open Punctuation

- Do not use punctuation after the salutation.
- Do not use punctuation after the complimentary closing.

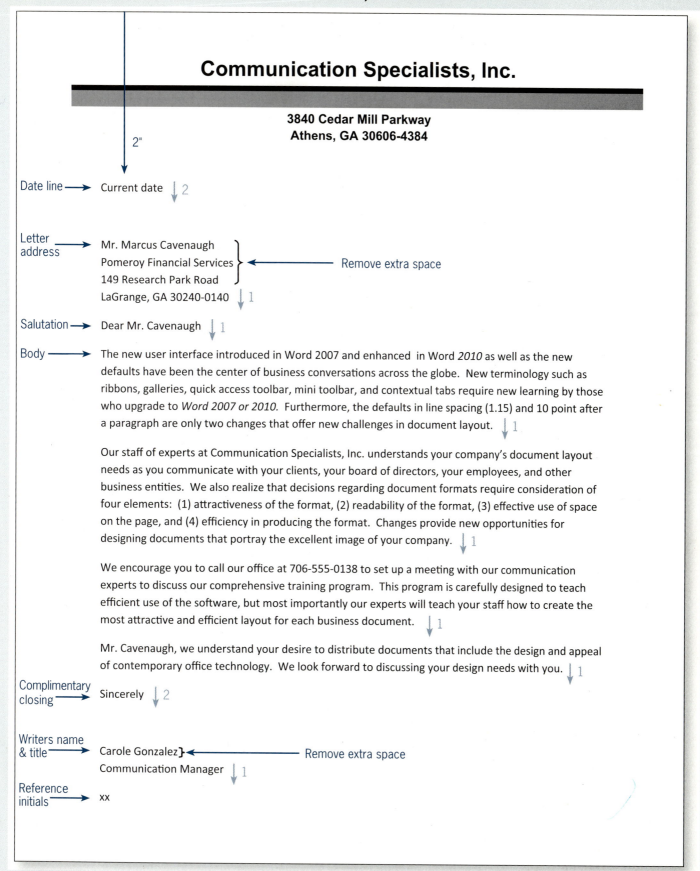

Communication Specialists, Inc.

3840 Cedar Mill Parkway
Athens, GA 30606-4384

2"

Date line → Current date ↓2

Letter address → Mr. Marcus Cavenaugh
Pomeroy Financial Services ← Remove extra space
149 Research Park Road
LaGrange, GA 30240-0140 ↓1

Salutation → Dear Mr. Cavenaugh ↓1

Body → The new user interface introduced in Word 2007 and enhanced in Word *2010* as well as the new defaults have been the center of business conversations across the globe. New terminology such as ribbons, galleries, quick access toolbar, mini toolbar, and contextual tabs require new learning by those who upgrade to *Word 2007 or 2010*. Furthermore, the defaults in line spacing (1.15) and 10 point after a paragraph are only two changes that offer new challenges in document layout. ↓1

Our staff of experts at Communication Specialists, Inc. understands your company's document layout needs as you communicate with your clients, your board of directors, your employees, and other business entities. We also realize that decisions regarding document formats require consideration of four elements: (1) attractiveness of the format, (2) readability of the format, (3) effective use of space on the page, and (4) efficiency in producing the format. Changes provide new opportunities for designing documents that portray the excellent image of your company. ↓1

We encourage you to call our office at 706-555-0138 to set up a meeting with our communication experts to discuss our comprehensive training program. This program is carefully designed to teach efficient use of the software, but most importantly our experts will teach your staff how to create the most attractive and efficient layout for each business document. ↓1

Mr. Cavenaugh, we understand your desire to distribute documents that include the design and appeal of contemporary office technology. We look forward to discussing your design needs with you. ↓1

Complimentary closing → Sincerely ↓2

Writers name & title → Carole Gonzalez} ← Remove extra space
Communication Manager ↓1

Reference initials → xx

Source: VanHuss, Forde, and Woo, *Keyboarding & Word Processing Essentials*, 18e, South-Western Cengage Learning, 2010.

1. Transcribe the Word Mastery terms from the Transcription CD.

2. Transcribe the five documents from the Transcription CD as described below. Key the documents in block letter style with open punctuation and use the current date.

   • Open Document 1 and use the letterhead for Robertson, Jones & McMillan Publishing Company.

   • Open Document 2 and use the letterhead for KBCM Radio Station.

   • Open Document 3 and use the letterhead for Robertson, Jones & McMillan Publishing Company.

   • Open Document 4 and use the letterhead for King Advertising.

   • Open Document 5 and use the letterhead for King Advertising.

3. When you have transcribed a document using the file from the Transcription CD, remember to use the *Save As* feature and a distinctive name as the file name for each document.

4. Spell-check, proofread, and submit all five documents to your instructor for approval.

CHAPTER CHECKPOINTS

Place a check mark beside the objectives you can meet after completing this chapter.

_____ I can define, spell, and use the Word Mastery terms in this chapter.

_____ I can use the commonly misused terms from the Word Usage section in this chapter.

_____ I can spell correctly the words in the Spelling section in this chapter.

_____ I can apply the rules for commas and capitalization presented in the Language Skills section in this chapter.

_____ I can transcribe documents in block letter style with open punctuation and proofread carefully.

*Evaluation Form

Access the Evaluation Form from your Transcription CD. Complete it and submit it with your work. You may choose to either print the form and complete it or complete the form electronically.

©auremar/Shutterstock.com

Chapter 3
EDUCATION, GOVERNMENT, AND PUBLIC SERVICE

The fields of education, government, and public service offer challenging careers that are rewarding, especially if you enjoy helping or serving others. Usually a bachelor's degree or master's degree is required for a teaching position. Teachers must be licensed in the state in which they are employed. Licensure programs are also required. Government and public service workers must have a high school diploma, and post-secondary training is also desired. Many positions require specialized training.

ENGLISH SKILLS REVIEW

 Word Mastery Preview

Directions: Review the list of Word Mastery terms that will be used in the documents you will be transcribing. Learn the definition for each word and how to spell it correctly.

principal	*Definition:*	head or director of a school
	Example:	The principal decided to hire three new teachers.
recommendation	*Definition:*	advice
	Example:	My recommendation would be to cancel the class.
credentials	*Definition:*	anything that provides the basis for confidence, belief, or credit
	Example:	We received his teaching credentials from the State Board of Education.
retention	*Definition:*	the act of retaining or keeping
	Example:	Our retention rate of students is very good this year.
probationary	*Definition:*	conditional
	Example:	Your contract is probationary until you have completed six months of teaching.
municipal	*Definition:*	pertaining to the local government—town or city
	Example:	Municipal bonds were sold last month.
constituent	*Definition:*	one who authorizes another to act for him/her as a representative; a client
	Example:	The constituents from Montana were not going to vote for their congressman again.
restraints	*Definition:*	the acts of controlling or holding back
	Example:	Restraints had to be made on her demands.
felonies	*Definition:*	crimes of grave character such as murder or burglary
	Example:	Felonies are committed every day in our state.
misdemeanor	*Definition:*	a transgression or offense less than a felony
	Example:	We cannot overlook even the smallest misdemeanor.

| subversive | Definition: | tending to overthrow an establishment |
| | Example: | Subversive behavior will not be tolerated in our nation. |

| appeal | Definition: | request for a review of a case or issue |
| | Example: | The defendant's attorney made an appeal to the Fifth Circuit Court of Appeals. |

| judgment | Definition: | the judicial decision of a cause in court |
| | Example: | You can appeal the judgment made in court. |

| prosecution | Definition: | the instituting and carrying out of legal proceedings against a person |
| | Example: | His prosecution could not be delayed any longer. |

| ordinance | Definition: | regulation |
| | Example: | There are municipal ordinances against this type of behavior. |

B Word Usage

Directions: Learn to spell and define these confusing words, which may occur within the documents you will be transcribing.

| advice | (noun) helpful information or counsel |
| advise | (verb) to give advice or counsel |

| all ready | (pronoun and adjective) a group is prepared |
| already | (adverb) before the time expected |

| capital | (adjective or noun) chief or main; a city that is the seat of government; an uppercase letter; a sum of money |
| capitol | (noun) building used by state legislature or by congress |

consul	(noun) a governmental official
council	(noun) an assembly
counsel	(verb or noun) to give advice; advice; attorney

| formally | (adverb) in a formal manner |
| formerly | (adverb) previously |

| its | (pronoun) belonging to it |
| it's | (pronoun) contraction of *it is* |

| principal | (adjective or noun) most important; head of a school; sum of money |
| principle | (noun) rule or guide |

 Spelling

Directions: Learn to spell these common words.

among

business

column

discipline

environment

exercise

fundamental

happiness

hierarchy

intelligence

marriage

necessary

official

political

similar

Language Skills

Directions: Enhance your language skills by reviewing basic grammar, punctuation, capitalization, number/figure style, abbreviation style, and word division rules. Study the rules and examples below.

Rule: Use a comma to set off the name of a city from the name of the state and the name of the state from the rest of the sentence.

Examples:
- We often visit Denver, Colorado, during the skiing season.
- Orlando, Florida, is a great family vacation place.

Rule: Use a comma to set off a series of three or more words, phrases, or clauses unless each word, phrase, or clause is separated by a conjunction. Be sure to put a comma before the last item in the series.

Examples:
- Jeremy, Doug, David, and Mark were chosen to play first string on the basketball team.
- Anna and Amy and Amanda are all names that begin with the same letter.

Rule: Use a comma to set off introductory words or phrases.

Examples:
- Consequently, we had to stop the meeting because the debate was so heated.
- Of course, we will go ahead with our presentation.

Rule: Use an apostrophe to form the possessive of nouns. For all singular nouns, add *'s*. For a plural noun not ending in *s*, add *'s*. For a plural noun ending in *s*, add an apostrophe after the *s*.

Examples:
- The secretary's desk was not as large as the boss's desk.
- All women's purses are on sale this week.
- Our sales associates' bonuses were larger than usual this year.

Rule: Nouns that precede numerals are capitalized except in the case of *page, paragraph, line, note, size,* and *verse.* Do not capitalize nouns when they follow numerals.

Examples:
- We will meet in Room 567 this afternoon to discuss the teachers' schedules.

- Don't you want to see the five rooms before you decide if the building is large enough to meet your needs?

ENGLISH SKILLS EXERCISES

A Word Mastery

Directions: Apply what you learned in the English Skills Review. Choose the correct word in the following sentences from those found in the Word Mastery Preview.

1. The committee did not want my _____ regarding the issue.

2. Most companies require a(n) _____ period for all new employees.

3. Her _____ was denied by the Supreme Court.

4. _____ for the crimes he committed was done quickly.

5. Although many _____ may be listed, some are never enforced.

6. Many people commit _____ every day.

7. She was arrested and will serve time for the _____ she committed.

8. If you want to teach school, you have to possess certain _____.

9. The _____ rate of the students in Mrs. Buck's class was excellent.

10. Do you plan to appeal the _____ the court rendered?

B Word Usage

Directions: Choose the correct word in each of the following sentences.

1. (It's, Its) time for us to begin class.

2. We have (already, all ready) heard that presentation.

3. Do you want my (advice, advise) or not?

Word Usage (continued)

4. Alice was (formally, formerly) introduced to her students.

5. I sought legal (consul, council, counsel) before I decided to press the issue.

6. As Marianna was leaving the (capital, capitol), she twisted her ankle in the hallway.

7. The (principal, principle) reason we want to ask you is because you are an authority in governmental issues.

8. Her father had invested a great deal of (capital, capitol) to help her begin her own business.

9. The student was referred to his (principal, principle) by his homeroom teacher.

10. The cat hurt (its, it's) paw on the rough surface.

C Spelling

Directions: Choose the correct spelling in each of the following sentences.

1. The (official, oficial) reason for the delay was never revealed to us.

2. Our neighbors' (marriage, marrige) was very (similer, similar, similiar) to ours.

3. (Discipline, descipline) is some times (nesessary, necessary) in the classroom.

4. There were several rumors spreading (among, amung) the many students.

5. The (politicial, political) (enviroment, environment) in Washington is very strained.

6. After participating in her (exersize, exercise) class, Cynthia returned to her office to work on (bisness, business).

7. Having great wealth, health, and (intelligense, intelligence) does not mean you have great (happyness, happiness).

8. Climbing the (heiarchy, hierarchy) in an office is almost as difficult as climbing a (colum, column).

9. What (fundimental, fundamental) beliefs do you cling to in life?

10. Being in (business, bussiness) for the first time, Susan relied on her mentor's advice.

D Language Skills

Directions: Use proofreaders' marks to make corrections in the following sentences. Write "Correct" by the sentence if no corrections are needed.

1. Portland Oregon is a beautiful city to visit.

2. Needless to say, we enjoy getting together and singing and dancing.

3. Our dinner included a salad an entrée and a dessert.

4. The Young Girls Department is located on floor 2.

5. He didn't like the men's ties that were on display.

6. We would like to visit Black Mountain, North Carolina because it is so scenic.

7. Incidentally will you be able to vote in the next election?

8. The boys, girls, and infants departments are on the lower level.

9. The womens and mens departments are on the top level of the store.

10. JoAnne, Nancy and Dru passed the teachers' exam the first time.

E Composition

1. Compose and key a paragraph applying the word mastery, word usage, spelling, and language skills you have studied.

2. Compose and key a second paragraph that uses two examples of apostrophes correctly.

3. Compose and key a third paragraph that describes a personal experience you have had relating to people in education, government, or public service. Submit all three paragraphs to your instructor.

F Research

1. Conduct research using the Internet, newspaper, and library or talk with individuals who are actually employed in the education, government, and public service fields to obtain information about the topics listed below. When searching online, go to the U.S. Bureau of Labor Statistics website at **www.bls.gov** and click on the **Publications** tab. Then click on the *Occupational Outlook Handbook* and **Index** links. Click on the first letter of the name of the field. (Example: Click on the letter *E* and scroll down the screen to find information on *education.*) You can also do an online search of the name of the field/industry followed by the words *career* or *training*. (Example: *educational career* or *educational training*)

   - What are the employment opportunities for office workers in education, government, or public service?

   - What are the advantages and/or disadvantages of employment in these fields?

   - What skills or characteristics are necessary for someone who wants to work in these fields?

   - What are the job titles or positions in these fields?

   - What are the salary ranges for positions in these fields?

   - What additional information did you learn during this research?

2. Compose a document by keying paragraphs that address the questions above. Add a meaningful title. Include your name and the date. Proofread, edit, and revise the paragraphs to correct all grammar and spelling errors. Print the document. Proofread it again and make any final changes before submitting it to your instructor.

The documents in this chapter will be keyed in modified block letter style with mixed punctuation. Review the proper format described below and on the next page.

Modified Block Letter Style

Page Settings:

- Use default 1″ top, side, and bottom margins.
- Use default 11-point Calibri font and 1.15 line spacing.
- Begin the date line and the closing lines at the center point of the page. Begin all other lines at the left margin.

Date Line:

- Position the date at about 2″. Begin at least 0.5″ below the letterhead.
- Set a left tab at 3.25″ and key the date.

Letter Address: Begin the letter address two lines below the date. Remove the extra space between the lines in the letter address.

Salutation: Key the salutation one line below the letter address.

Body: Begin the body one line below the salutation.

Complimentary Closing:

- Position the complimentary closing one line below the body.
- Begin keying at 3.25″.

Writer's Name and Title:

- Begin the writer's name and title two lines below the closing.
- Begin keying at 3.25″.

Reference Initials: Key the reference initials in lowercase one line below the the writer's name/title.

Mixed Punctuation

- Key a colon after the salutation.
- Key a comma after the complimentary closing.

Modified Block Letter with Mixed Punctuation

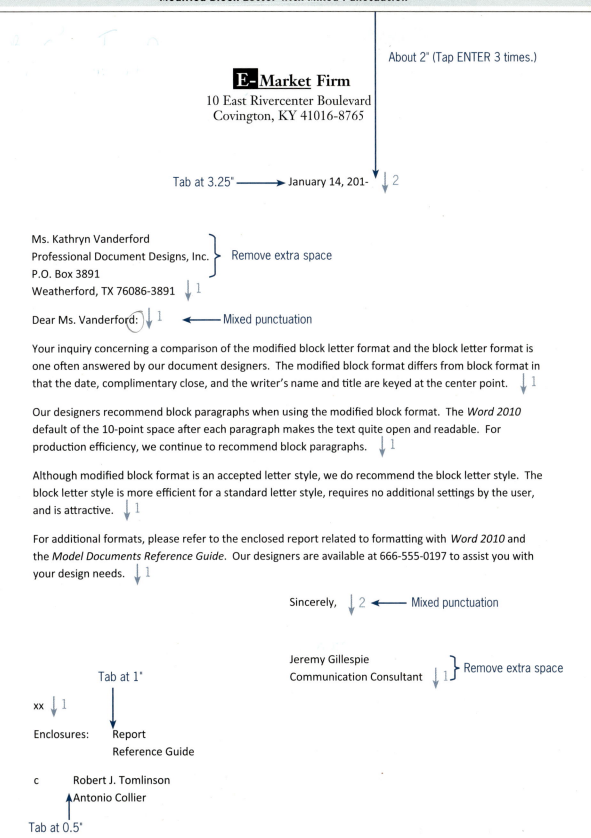

About 2" (Tap ENTER 3 times.)

E-Market Firm
10 East Rivercenter Boulevard
Covington, KY 41016-8765

Tab at 3.25" ——→ January 14, 201- ↓2

Ms. Kathryn Vanderford
Professional Document Designs, Inc. ⎫ Remove extra space
P.O. Box 3891
Weatherford, TX 76086-3891 ↓1

Dear Ms. Vanderford: ↓1 ←—— Mixed punctuation

Your inquiry concerning a comparison of the modified block letter format and the block letter format is one often answered by our document designers. The modified block format differs from block format in that the date, complimentary close, and the writer's name and title are keyed at the center point. ↓1

Our designers recommend block paragraphs when using the modified block format. The *Word 2010* default of the 10-point space after each paragraph makes the text quite open and readable. For production efficiency, we continue to recommend block paragraphs. ↓1

Although modified block format is an accepted letter style, we do recommend the block letter style. The block letter style is more efficient for a standard letter style, requires no additional settings by the user, and is attractive. ↓1

For additional formats, please refer to the enclosed report related to formatting with *Word 2010* and the *Model Documents Reference Guide*. Our designers are available at 666-555-0197 to assist you with your design needs. ↓1

Sincerely, ↓2 ←—— Mixed punctuation

Jeremy Gillespie
Communication Consultant ↓1 ⎫ Remove extra space

Tab at 1"

xx ↓1

Enclosures: Report
               Reference Guide

c   Robert J. Tomlinson
       Antonio Collier

Tab at 0.5"

Source: VanHuss, Forde, and Woo, *Keyboarding & Word Processing Essentials*, 18e, South-Western Cengage Learning, 2010.

1. Transcribe the Word Mastery terms from the Transcription CD.

2. Transcribe the five documents from the Transcription CD as described below. Key the documents in modified block style with mixed punctuation and use the current date.

    - Open Document 1 and use the letterhead for Brookwood Community College.

    - Open Document 2 and use the letterhead for Mayor Jerome Jordan.

    - Open Document 3 and use the letterhead for Kingsbury Police Department.

    - Open Document 4 and use the letterhead for Kingsbury Police Department.

    - Open Document 5 and use the letterhead for Brookwood Community College.

3. When you have transcribed a document using the file from the Transcription CD, remember to use the **Save As** feature and a distinctive name as the file name for each document.

4. Spell-check, proofread, and submit all five documents to your instructor for approval.

CHAPTER CHECKPOINTS

Place a check mark beside the objectives you can meet after completing this chapter.

_____ I can define, spell, and use the Word Mastery terms in this chapter.

_____ I can use the commonly misused terms from the Word Usage section in this chapter.

_____ I can spell correctly the words in the Spelling section in this chapter.

_____ I can apply the rules for commas, apostrophes, and capitalization presented in the Language Skills section in this chapter.

_____ I can transcribe documents in modified block letter style with mixed punctuation and proofread carefully.

✳ Evaluation Form

Access the Evaluation Form from your Transcription CD. Complete it and submit it with your work. You may choose to either print the form and complete it or complete the form electronically.

Chapter 4
REAL ESTATE, APPRAISING, AND PROPERTY MANAGEMENT

The field of real estate, appraising, and property management appeals to those individuals who like to sell or manage various types of property. The two basic types of property are commercial, referring to properties for business and industry, and residential, referring to real estate for private individuals. Most positions require a high school diploma, and post-secondary training is desirable. Specialized training and licensing is required to sell and appraise property.

LEARNING OBJECTIVES

After completing all the learning activities in this chapter, you will be able to:

- Define, spell, and use the Word Mastery terms.

- Use commonly misused words appropriately.

- Use correct spelling for commonly misspelled words.

- Apply the rules for semicolons, commas, and hyphens presented in this chapter.

- Apply the rules for numbers/figures presented in this chapter.

- Apply proofreading and transcription skills.

- Transcribe documents in various letter and memorandum formats.

A Word Mastery Preview

Directions: Review the list of Word Mastery terms that will be used in the documents you will be transcribing. Learn the definition for each word and how to spell it correctly.

available	*Definition:*	suitable or ready
	Example:	Your new property will be available next month.
opportunity	*Definition:*	a chance
	Example:	We hope you will take advantage of this opportunity to increase your knowledge of the subject.
townhouse	*Definition:*	a group of homes that are joined by common walls
	Example:	Unfortunately, the fire that occurred in one townhouse caused damage to the other townhouses as well.
ranch home	*Definition:*	any house with one story
	Example:	Many older people prefer ranch homes instead of two-story homes.
relocation	*Definition:*	the process of moving
	Example:	Relocation from one state to another can be expensive.
client	*Definition:*	a customer
	Example:	Be sure to give your client excellent customer service.
commercial property	*Definition:*	land or buildings for business use
	Example:	Commercial property is very expensive.
residential property	*Definition:*	land or buildings for one's own home
	Example:	With the new subdivision that has been developed, there will be more residential property available.
wheelchair-accessible	*Definition:*	designed for wheelchair mobility
	Example:	All businesses must have wheelchair-accessible entrances.
lease	*Definition:*	rent
	Example:	I would like to lease the building for my new business.

| approximately | *Definition:* | nearly exact |
| | *Example:* | Unfortunately, the trip was approximately one hour longer than we had expected. |

| licensee | *Definition:* | a person to whom a license has been issued or granted |
| | *Example:* | The contract was given to the licensee. |

| brokerage | *Definition:* | a business that sells or buys things for a commission |
| | *Example:* | The brokerage company will charge a fee for selling your home. |

| fiduciary | *Definition:* | trustworthy |
| | *Example:* | Fiduciary transactions should be the goal of every business. |

| confidentiality | *Definition:* | the act of keeping something private |
| | *Example:* | Confidentiality applies to all business transactions. |

| disclosure | *Definition:* | the act of revealing |
| | *Example:* | The disclosure statement listed the structural problems with the building. |

| diligence | *Definition:* | persistent or constant effort |
| | *Example:* | Diligence and time are sometimes required in selling property. |

| pertinent | *Definition:* | relevant or relating to the matter at hand |
| | *Example:* | We must be sure to include all pertinent information in the contract. |

B Word Usage

Directions: Learn to spell and define these confusing words, which may occur within the documents you will be transcribing.

| addition | (noun) the act of joining one thing to another |
| edition | (noun) a version of a publication |

| any time | (noun) no particular time (preceded by the word *at*); any amount of time |
| anytime | (adverb) no particular time (never preceded by the word *at*) |

| appraise | (verb) to set a value on |
| apprize | (verb) to inform |

Word Usage (*continued*)

complement	(noun or verb) something that adds or completes another; to complete
compliment	(verb or noun) to praise; a flattering comment

large	(adjective) used to describe one person or thing as being big in size
larger	(adjective) used to compare two persons or things as being big in size
largest	(adjective) used to compare more than two persons or things as being big in size

than	(conjuction) compared to
then	(adverb) at that time

weather	(noun) atmospheric conditions
whether	(conjunction) used with one of two possibilities

Spelling

Directions: Learn to spell these common words.

accommodate	explanation	pursue
careful	guarantee	recommend
ceiling	interesting	temporary
congratulate	leisure	transferred
eighth	occurred	unnecessary

Language Skills

Directions: Enhance your language skills by reviewing basic grammar, punctuation, capitalization, number/figure style, abbreviation style, and word division rules. Study the rules and examples below.

Rule:	Use a semicolon between two closely related independent clauses that are not joined by a conjunction.
Examples:	• I often enjoy reading a good book; I don't watch much television.
	• Homes on this block sell fast; homes two blocks away do not sell as fast.

Rule:	Use a comma to separate two independent clauses that are joined by the conjunctions *and, but, or,* and *nor.* The comma is placed before the conjunction.
Examples:	• I left the office very quickly, and I must have forgotten my briefcase.
	• Nathan and Karen wanted to buy a new home, but they were unable to save enough money.

Rule: Use a comma to separate two adjectives that are of equal rank and modify the same noun. The word *and* could be placed between these adjectives, and the sentence would still read correctly.

Examples:
- The intelligent, beautiful woman was her daughter.
- He completed the complicated, lengthy document.

Rule: Use a hyphen to join compound adjectives before a noun they modify as a unit. The word *and* cannot be placed between these adjectives because the sentence would not read correctly.

Examples:
- The well-known author died last month.
- Natalie owned a fast-growing accounting firm.

Rule: Spell out the house number *one* and use figures for all other house numbers. Spell out numbers *ten* and below used for the names of streets; use figures for numbers above *ten* used as street names.

Examples:
- His new office is located at One Ninth Avenue.
- His home is located at 27 East 12th Avenue.

ENGLISH SKILLS EXERCISES

A Word Mastery

Directions: Apply what you learned in the English Skills Review. Choose the correct word in the following sentences from those found in the Word Mastery Preview.

1. I do not know when my employer will be _____ to take your call.

2. A new _____ will be contacting me about the sale of her home.

3. _____ three new employees will be hired.

4. Because she gave the bank her personal information when applying for the loan, _____ in this matter must be upheld.

5. If you want to succeed, you will have to use _____ in pursuing your goal.

6. When an excellent _____ arises to buy the home you want, you should take advantage of it.

Word Mastery (continued)

7. _____ from one branch office to another often occurs in today's business world.

8. Many businesses _____ their office buildings rather than purchase them.

9. All _____ information should be disclosed to the buyers.

10. Not all businesses conduct ____fiduciary____ transactions.

B Word Usage

Directions: Choose the correct word in each of the following sentences.

1. Why don't you come see me (anytime, any time) that is convenient for you?

2. My realtor said that he could (appraise, apprize) me as to the amount I should list my house.

3. Men like to hear a (complement, compliment) as much as women do.

4. When you compare the size of my home to your home, your home is (large, larger, largest).

5. What is the (weather, whether) going to be like tomorrow?

6. My parents decided to add an (edition, addition) to their home.

7. My wife liked the new home more (than, then) I did.

8. I asked my realtor to (appraise, apprize) my home before I decide whether or not I really want to sell it.

9. At (anytime, any time) we could be asked to provide more information.

10. That color will (complement, compliment) your hair and skin tones nicely.

C Spelling

Directions: Choose the correct spelling in each of the following sentences.

1. During my (leisure, leizure) time, I like to play card games.

2. My friends wanted to (congratulate, congradulate) me when they saw me (pursue, persue) and win the prize.

3. Wilson will (recommend, reccommend) an (interesting, intiresting) opportunity to you next week.

4. The (celing, ceiling) paint is just (temperary, temporary); we plan to have it painted again in a different color.

5. When we sold our home, we (transfered, transferred) the termite (guaranty, guarantee).

6. John wanted to (acommodate, accommodate) his son's needs.

7. If you will take a (careful, carefull) look at the floor, you will notice it has several small dents.

8. What (explaination, explanation) do you have regarding when the accident (occured, occurred)?

9. Can you believe that Kate had her (eighth, eigth) child?

10. His comments were totally (unnecesary, unnecessary).

D Language Skills

Directions: Use proofreaders' marks to make corrections in the following sentences. Write "Correct" by the sentence if no corrections are needed.

1. Some people prefer to work during the day some people prefer to work at night.

2. I don't know the answer to the question but I am sure Susan could provide the information you need.

3. The middle aged woman did not look a day over thirty.

4. Many people desire an exciting rewarding career.

5. 1 Main Street was his old address 14 5th Avenue will be his new address after the first of the year.

6. Everyone wants to own his or her own home but everyone cannot afford to do so.

7. If you want a well built house, be sure to select a good builder.

8. She used to live on 8th Street.

9. Carmen is an excellent well trained realtor.

10. We moved from 22nd Avenue last year.

E Composition

1. Compose and key a paragraph applying the word mastery, word usage, spelling, and language skills you have studied.

2. Compose and key a second paragraph that explains the importance of confidentiality in a business setting.

3. Compose and key a third paragraph that explains when figures should be used in addresses and when they should be spelled out rather than written in figure form. Submit all three paragraphs to your instructor.

F Research

1. Conduct research using the Internet, newspaper, and library or talk with individuals who are actually employed in the real estate, appraising, and property management fields to obtain information about the topics listed below. When searching online, go to the U.S. Bureau of Labor Statistics

Research (*continued*)

website at **www.bls.gov** and click on the **Publications** tab. Then click on the *Occupational Outlook Handbook* and **Index** links. Click on the first letter of the name of the field. (Example: Click on the letter *R* and scroll down the screen to find information on *real estate*.) You can also do an online search of the name of the field/industry followed by the words *career* or *training*. (Example: *real estate career* or *real estate training*)

- What are the employment opportunities for office workers in real estate, appraising, or property management?

- What are the advantages and/or disadvantages of employment in these fields?

- What skills or characteristics are necessary for someone who wants to work in these fields?

- What are the job titles or positions in these fields?

- What are the salary ranges for positions in these fields?

- What additional information did you learn during this research?

2. Compose a document by keying paragraphs that address the questions above. Add a meaningful title. Include your name and the date. Proofread, edit, and revise the paragraphs to correct all grammar and spelling errors. Print the document. Proofread it again and make any final changes before submitting it to your instructor.

TRANSCRIPTION PREVIEW

In this chapter, some documents will be keyed in block letter style and some in modified block letter style. Some will be keyed with open punctuation and some with mixed punctuation. Be sure to review these formats in the Transcription Preview sections in Chapters 2 and 3 or in the reference manual in the back of this text-workbook. You also will be keying memorandums in this chapter. Review the proper format for memorandums described below and on the next page.

Memorandum Format

- Use default 1″ top, side, and bottom margins.

- Use default 11-point Calibri font and 1.15 line spacing.

- Tap ENTER three times to position the first line of the heading at about 2″.

- Format the headings (TO, FROM, DATE, and SUBJECT) in bold and uppercase.

- Tap the TAB once or twice after each heading so the text is aligned. Be sure to turn off bold and uppercase before keying the text.

- Tap ENTER once after each heading to key the next heading.

- Tap ENTER once after each paragraph.

- Tap ENTER once after the last paragraph and key your reference initals.

Sterling

1195 Singing Cactus Avenue
Tucson, AZ 85701-0947

2" (Tap ENTER three times.)

TO: Students ↓1

FROM: Madison Pietrzak, Communication Consultant ↓1

DATE: Current date ↓1

SUBJECT: A Business Perspective on Memos ↓1

This memo was requested by your keyboarding instructor for the purpose of describing the changing role of memos and the importance of formatting memos effectively. Sterling uses its logo and company name on the top of its memos. First, you will learn to prepare memos on plain paper. Later you will learn to use templates for them. A template is a stored document format that would contain the company logo and name as well as the memo headings. ↓1

The format does not differ regardless of whether plain paper or a template is used. The headings are positioned about 2" from the top of the paper, and default side margins are used. Headings are keyed in uppercase and bold; tap the ENTER key once after each heading. The body is single-spaced with a blank line between each paragraph. Notations such as reference initials, enclosures, or copies are keyed one blank line below the body. Some companies adopt slightly different styles; however, this style is very commonly used. ↓1

Often a memo is sent electronically. It can either be in the form of an e-mail or as an attachment to an e-mail. Memos were designed to be documents that stayed within a company. However, e-mail is changing the role of memos. E-mails, even though they are formatted as memos, are frequently sent outside of companies. Some companies use e-mail to deliver a document but attach a letter or a memo to it. ↓1

xx ← Student's first and last initials

Source: VanHuss, Forde, and Woo, *Keyboarding & Word Processing Essentials*, 18e, South-Western Cengage Learning, 2010.

TRANSCRIPTION EXERCISES

1. Transcribe the Word Mastery terms from the Transcription CD.

2. Transcribe the five documents from the Transcription CD following the instructions below and using the current date.

   - Open Document 1 and use the letterhead for Jefferson Real Estate Company. Key this in block letter style with mixed punctuation.

   - Open Document 2 and use the letterhead for Jefferson Real Estate Company. Key this in memorandum format.

   - Open Document 3 and use the letterhead for Becker Residential Property Management. Key this in modified block style with open punctuation.

   - Open Document 4 and use the letterhead for Chicago Commercial Property Management Incorporated. Key this in memorandum format.

   - Open Document 5 and use the letterhead for Becker Residential Property Management. Key this in modified block style with mixed punctuation.

3. When you have transcribed a document using the file from the Transcription CD, remember to use the *Save As* feature and a distinctive name as the file name for each document.

4. Spell-check, proofread, and submit all five documents to your instructor for approval.

CHAPTER CHECKPOINTS

Place a check mark beside the objectives
you can meet after completing this chapter.

_____ I can define, spell, and use the Word Mastery terms in this chapter.

_____ I can use the commonly misused terms from the Word Usage section in
this chapter.

_____ I can spell correctly the words in the Spelling section in this chapter.

_____ I can apply the rules for semicolons, commas, and hyphens presented in
the Language Skills section in this chapter.

_____ I can apply the rules for number/figure style presented in the Language
Skills section in this chapter.

_____ I can transcribe documents in various letter and memorandum formats
and proofread carefully.

Evaluation Form

Access the Evaluation Form from your Transcription CD. Complete it and
submit it with your work. You may choose to either print the form and
complete it or complete the form electronically.

© Alexander Kalina/Shutterstock.com

Chapter 5

ACCOUNTING, AUDITING, AND FINANCIAL PLANNING

The fields of accounting, auditing, and financial planning offer careers for those individuals who are detail-oriented and enjoy working with numbers. Post-secondary education and certification may be required. A master's degree and knowledge of computer software are desired.

ENGLISH SKILLS REVIEW

 A **Word Mastery Preview**

Directions: Review the list of Word Mastery terms that will be used in the documents you will be transcribing. Learn the definition for each word and how to spell it correctly.

examination
Definition: the act of investigating or inspecting
Example: An examination of her report must be implemented.

financial
Definition: pertaining to money matters
Example: Financial reports are required by businesses.

retained
Definition: held in place
Example: Her earnings were retained by her agent.

accordance
Definition: agreement
Example: We followed his directions in accordance with the list he gave us.

auditing
Definition: the act of verifying financial records
Example: The auditing process revealed numerous errors in their accounts.

conformity
Definition: acting according to certain accepted standards
Example: Many young people find conformity very confining.

taxpayer
Definition: a person who is subject to paying tax
Example: Many taxpayers wait until the last minute to submit their tax returns.

recipients
Definition: a person or thing that receives
Example: She gave away her money to several recipients.

Internal Revenue Service
Definition: the agency that is responsible for enforcing tax laws and collecting tax payments
Example: He was hired to be an auditor for the Internal Revenue Service.

B Word Usage

Directions: Learn to spell and define these confusing words, which may occur within the documents you will be transcribing.

ad	(noun) an advertisement
add	(verb) to find the sum
fiscal	(adjective) relating to financial matters
physical	(adjective) pertaining to the body
personal	(adjective) private
personnel	(noun) employees
perspective	(noun) the ability to see things in correct proportion
prospective	(adjective) likely to come about
quiet	(adjective, noun, or verb) not noisy; silence; to calm down
quit	(verb) to stop
quite	(adverb) entirely
sure	(adjective) confident; convinced
surely	(adverb) certainly; without a doubt
thorough	(adjective) carried through to completion
through	(preposition) from beginning to end; by means of or because of

C Spelling

Directions: Learn to spell these common words.

acquire	**forty**	**separate**
address	**independent**	**twelfth**
certain	**privilege**	**using**
definite	**questionnaire**	**usually**
exaggerate	**secretary**	**welfare**

D Language Skills

Directions: Enhance your language skills by reviewing basic grammar, punctuation, capitalization, number/figure style, abbreviation style, and word division rules. Study the rules and examples below.

Rule:	Use a comma to set off a prepositional phrase of four or more words at the beginning of a sentence. Do not use a comma to set off a prepositional phrase of less than four words. Although "of

course" is a prepositional phrase, it is considered a parenthetical expression and is always set off by commas.

Examples:
- In the first meeting, we elected officers.
- In June we will get married.

Rule: Use a comma to set off the name of a person you are directly addressing.

Examples:
- Dr. Evans, will you be able to attend the conference?
- Please open the door, Alice.
- If you will give us the information, Mr. Jones, we can process your application.

Rule: Use a semicolon before a conjunction joining two independent clauses if either clause contains one or more commas.

Examples:
- Lakisha is an excellent student; and she, of course, is well liked by all her classmates.
- In the beginning of the course, Matt did not like accounting; but he now has decided he wants to become a certified public accountant.

Rule: Use a semicolon before a transitional adverb that joins two independent clauses. A comma follows the adverb.

Examples:
- She purchased the text-workbook; therefore, she will be able to read the homework assignment.
- Math was not Nathan's best subject in college; however, he has used math extensively in his mortgage lending position.

Rule: Some professional titles are abbreviated; some professional designations are written without periods, but academic degrees require periods.

Examples:
- Sandra Smith, R.N., Cheryl Sheffel, CPA, and John Adams, M.D., were at the banquet.
- Dr. John Smith will see Rick Warren, CFP, for his financial planning.
- Selena Gomez received her M.Ed. last year when her husband, Jose Gomez, received his Ph.D.

ENGLISH SKILLS EXERCISES

A Word Mastery

Directions: Apply what you learned in the English Skills Review. Choose the correct word in the following sentences from those found in the Word Mastery Preview.

1. Of course, our _____ was completed in detail.
2. His ___financial___ records were not very accurate.
3. We performed our work in ___accordance___ with the instructions given to us.
4. The ___recipient___ of the award thanked the audience.
5. By April 15 most people mail their tax returns to the _____.
6. His earnings were ___returned___ per his instructions.
7. When the ___auditing___ process began, many in the accounting department were anxious.
8. Most ___taxpayers___ don't enjoy paying taxes.
9. The accounting practices were in ___accordance___ with the regulations they were to follow.
10. Most businesses are required to provide ___financial___ reports to their investors.

B Word Usage

Directions: Choose the correct word in each of the following sentences.

1. We know you will (sure, surely) handle our tax prepartion properly.
2. Since we know how (thorough, through) you are with every detail, you are the person we want to handle our financial planning.
3. The (ad, add) stated that the chairs were on sale for $125 each.
4. Please (quiet, quit, quite) smoking in this area and go to the designated area if you must smoke.
5. Jim had his (fiscal, physical) at the doctor's office yesterday and was shocked to learn that he needed to lose 25 pounds.
6. At the end of the (fiscal, physical) year, we will know whether or not we need to (ad, add) more employees.
7. Most people consider their financial information to be very (personal, personnel).
8. From our accountant's (perspective, prospective), she thinks we will get a greater refund this year than we did last year.
9. If you are going to do your taxes yourself, be sure to work in a (quiet, quit, quite) place so you can give your full attention to the task at hand.
10. (Personal, Personnel) in the company have all had concerns as to how the economy will affect their employment.

C Spelling

Directions: Choose the correct spelling in each of the following sentences.

1. The company recently used an (independant, independent) employment agency to help it hire the president's new (secretery, secretary).

2. If you will complete the (questionaire, questionnaire), it will only take 15 minutes.

3. We are not (useing, using) the same person to prepare our taxes that we used last year.

4. The (wellfare, welfare) of my children will be affected by the actions your company takes.

5. There is a (difinite, definite) (priviledge, privilege) to home ownership.

6. (Useually, Usually) we do not ask people to give us their mailing (adress, address) when they submit the information we requested.

7. I did not (exaggerate, exasserate) when I said that there were over (fourty, forty) people at the open house last week.

8. Their new office will be located on the (twelveth, twelfth) floor.

9. When you are (certain, sertain) that you know the answer, you may raise your hand.

10. John and Susan did not (acquire, aquire) the needed information to help them make the decision that had to be made.

D Language Skills

Directions: Use proofreaders' marks to make corrections in the following sentences. Write "Correct" by the sentence if no corrections are needed.

1. In the spring we will plant our garden.

2. In the early chapters you will learn the rules for using commas.

3. Our class will meet Monday Wednesday and Friday but we will not have class on Tuesday and Thursday.

4. Now is the time to pursue your goals therefore start writing down what you hope to achieve this year.

5. We would like to hear your report doctor Joseph on the benefits of exercise.

6. Sarah Katherine please give the accountant the information he requested.

7. Of course, we can get your tax return processed before the deadline and we will charge you our normal fee.

8. On your last year's tax return we did not list your social security number correctly.

9. In today's history class we received our test scores.

10. I do not like math therefore I would probably not enjoy the accounting profession.

E Composition

1. Compose and key a paragraph applying the word mastery, word usage, spelling, and language skills you have studied.

2. Compose and key a second paragraph that explains how mathematics can be helpful to you in life even if you don't plan to pursue a career in accounting, auditing, or financial planning.

3. Compose and key a third paragraph that describes how you manage your own personal finances. Submit all three paragraphs to your instructor.

F Research

1. Conduct research using the Internet, newspaper, and library or talk with individuals who are actually employed in the accounting, auditing, and financial planning fields to obtain information about the topics listed below. When searching online, go to the U.S. Bureau of Labor Statistics website at **www.bls.gov** and click on the **Publications** tab. Then click on the *Occupational Outlook Handbook* and **Index** links. Click on the first letter of the name of the field. (Example: Click on the letter *A* and scroll down the screen to find information on *accounting*.) You can also do an online search of the name of the field/industry followed by the words *career* or *training*. (Example: *accounting career* or *accounting training*)

   • What are the employment opportunities for office workers in the accounting, auditing, and financial planning fields?

   • What are the advantages and/or disadvantages of employment in these fields?

   • What skills or characteristics are necessary for someone who wants to work in these fields?

   • What are the job titles or positions in these fields?

   • What are the salary ranges for positions in these fields?

   • What additional information did you learn during this research?

2. Compose a document by keying paragraphs that address the questions above. Add a meaningful title. Include your name and the date. Proofread, edit, and revise the paragraphs to correct all grammar and spelling errors. Print the document. Proofread it again and make any final changes before submitting it to your instructor.

Subject lines may be used in letters to let the reader know the topic of the communication. Review the proper format for subject lines described below.

Subject Lines

- Tap Enter once after the salutation and key the subject line by capitalizing all letters or by capitalizing the first letter of each major word.

- The subject line may or may not be preceded by the word *Subject* and a colon followed by two spaces.

- Tap Enter once after the subject line to begin the body of your letter.

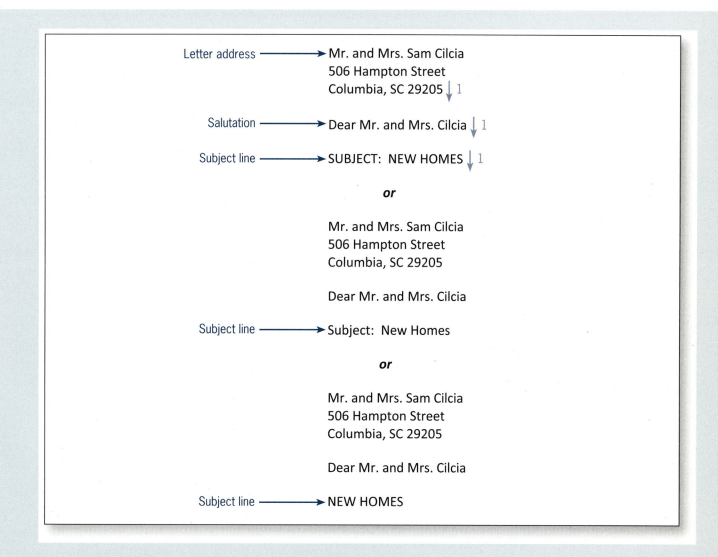

Letter address ⟶ Mr. and Mrs. Sam Cilcia
506 Hampton Street
Columbia, SC 29205 ↓ 1

Salutation ⟶ Dear Mr. and Mrs. Cilcia ↓ 1

Subject line ⟶ SUBJECT: NEW HOMES ↓ 1

or

Mr. and Mrs. Sam Cilcia
506 Hampton Street
Columbia, SC 29205

Dear Mr. and Mrs. Cilcia

Subject line ⟶ Subject: New Homes

or

Mr. and Mrs. Sam Cilcia
506 Hampton Street
Columbia, SC 29205

Dear Mr. and Mrs. Cilcia

Subject line ⟶ NEW HOMES

1. Transcribe the Word Mastery terms from the Transcription CD.

2. Transcribe the five documents from the Transcription CD following the instructions below and using the current date.

   - Open Document 1 and use the letterhead for Private Accounts, Inc. Key this document in block letter style with open punctuation.

   - Open Document 2 and use the letterhead for Private Accounts, Inc. Key this document in block letter style with open punctuation.

   - Open Document 3 and use the letterhead for Coburn-Fisk Financial Planners, Inc. Key this document in block letter style with open punctuation.

   - Open Document 4 and use the Instructions for Filing form. Key the information dictated in the appropriate spaces on the form.

   - Open Document 5 and use the Instructions for Filing form. Key the information dictated in the appropriate spaces on the form.

3. When you have transcribed a document using the file from the Transcription CD, remember to use the *Save As* feature and a distinctive name as the file name for each document.

4. Spell-check, proofread, and submit all five documents to your instructor for approval.

CHAPTER CHECKPOINTS

Place a check mark beside the objectives you can meet after completing this chapter.

_____ I can define, spell, and use the Word Mastery terms in this chapter.

_____ I can use the commonly misused terms from the Word Usage section in this chapter.

_____ I can spell correctly the words in the Spelling section in this chapter.

_____ I can apply the rules for commas, semicolons, and abbreviations presented in the Language Skills section in this chapter.

_____ I can transcribe documents containing subject lines and proofread carefully.

_____ I can transcribe documents by keying information into financial forms and proofread carefully.

Evaluation Form

Access the Evaluation Form from your Transcription CD. Complete it and submit it with your work. You may choose to either print the form and complete it or complete the form electronically.

Chapter 6

BANKING, FINANCIAL MANAGEMENT, AND CONSUMER CREDIT

The fields of banking, financial management, and consumer credit can be demanding but offer fulfilling careers especially if you enjoy analytical work. A bachelor's degree or master's degree is usually required.

LEARNING OBJECTIVES

After completing all the learning activities in this chapter, you will be able to:

- Define, spell, and use the Word Mastery terms.

- Use commonly misused words appropriately.

- Use correct spelling for commonly misspelled words.

- Apply the rules for commas presented in this chapter.

- Apply the rules for number/figure style presented in this chapter.

- Apply proofreading and transcription skills.

- Transcribe documents containing enclosure notations.

Word Mastery Preview

Directions: Review the list of Word Mastery terms that will be used in the documents you will be transcribing. Learn the definition for each word and how to spell it correctly.

certificate	*Definition:*	a document serving as evidence
	Example:	We have many certificates to prove our claim.
investment	*Definition:*	money that has been put to use in order to return a profit
	Example:	My investment was not a very wise one.
opportunities	*Definition:*	situations or conditions favorable for attainment of a goal
	Example:	Many people have not had the opportunities you have had to earn a degree.
deposits	*Definition:*	money placed in a bank
	Example:	Our bank does accept night deposits.
draft	*Definition:*	to draw out funds
	Example:	We can draft your account each month for your house payment.
CDs	*Definition:*	abbreviation for Certificate of Deposit; financial instruments issued by the bank that earn interest on the money deposited
	Example:	She has purchased several CDs in the past few years.
yielding	*Definition:*	the act of producing
	Example:	His investments are yielding a good return.
IRA	*Definition:*	abbreviation for Individual Retirement Account; a method of investing that produces savings that will not be withdrawn until retirement
	Example:	Both he and his wife decided to set up an IRA as one way to save for their future.
payee	*Definition:*	a person to whom money is paid
	Example:	She wrote his name as the payee for her check.

| **insufficient** | *Definition:* | not enough |
| | *Example:* | There were insufficient funds on deposit at the bank. |

| **service charge** | *Definition:* | a fee charged by a bank for providing a particular service |
| | *Example:* | Brandon was not aware that a service charge would be assessed by the bank. |

| **cashier's check** | *Definition:* | a check drawn by a bank on its own funds and signed by its cashier |
| | *Example:* | Only accept a cashier's check or cash when you sell your car. |

| **overdraft** | *Definition:* | a draft in excess of one's balance |
| | *Example:* | An overdraft on your account could result in checks being returned. |

| **money market account** | *Definition:* | a type of savings account that earns interest and permits a limited number of withdrawals |
| | *Example:* | Tenisha opened her first money market account at her local bank. |

 ## Word Usage

Directions: Learn to spell and define these confusing words, which may occur within the documents you will be transcribing.

| **among** | (preposition) used with more than two people or things |
| **between** | (preposition) used with two people or things |

| **buy** | (verb) to purchase |
| **by** | (preposition) through; with; no later than |

| **cease** | (verb) stop |
| **seize** | (verb) take control of |

| **disinterested** | (adjective) neutral; not biased |
| **uninterested** | (adjective) not concerned with; lacking interest |

less	(adjective) used to describe one person or thing as being insignificant
lesser	(adjective) used in comparing two persons or things as being insignificant
least	(adjective) used in comparing more than two persons or things as being insignificant

Word Usage (*continued*)

real	(adjective) genuine or true
really	(adverb) truly or actually

weak	(adjective) pathetic or fragile
week	(noun) seven days

C Spelling

Directions: Learn to spell these common words.

acceptable	exceed	successful
balance	misspell	through
believe	ninth	until
criticize	planning	unusual
difference	precede	withhold

D Language Skills

Directions: Enhance your language skills by reviewing basic grammar, punctuation, capitalization, number/figure style, abbreviation style, and word division rules. Study the rules and examples below.

Rule: Use a comma to separate a date from the year and the year from the rest of the sentence.

Examples:
- On August 31, 2012, he will celebrate his twenty-first birthday.
- He was born on April 21, 2005.

Rule: Except in formal or legal writing, the day of the month and the year are usually written in figures. When the date appears in the body of a letter, the year is customarily omitted if it is the same as that which appears on the dateline. It is not necessary to use *st*, *d*, or *th* in dates unless the day is written before or is separated from the month.

Examples:
- He turned 50 on January 4, 2011.
- She will celebrate her birthday on the 31st of March.

Rule: Use a comma to separate two unrelated numbers that are beside each other in a sentence.

Examples:
- In the year 2010, 50 different groups supported his cause.
- On May 12, 13 students were absent.

Rule: Percentages are written in figures followed by the word *percent*. The % symbol is used in tables and statistical data.

Examples:
- We need 25 percent of your report next week.
- Tom estimated that 2 percent of the students were sick on the first day of class.

Rule: Amounts of money, except in legal documents, are written in figures. Amounts less than one dollar are written in figures with the word *cents* following. In writing even sums of money, omit the decimal and double zeros.

Examples:
- Our check for $49.52 was mailed today.
- The customer was charged 50 cents for the gum.
- He was charged $5 for the binder he purchased.

Rule: Use figures for numbers that follow an identifying noun. Use words for numbers that precede the identifying noun unless the number is above ten. Use words for numbers that begin a sentence. If the term *number* precedes a figure, use the abbreviation *No.*

Examples:
- Please read pages 21 to 35 in your text-workbook.
- She opened the 13 letters that were on her desk.
- Eleven students will work together to prepare the five pages for the report due next week.
- We ordered three boxes of No. 10 envelopes for the office.

Proofreading
Tip

- If you are keying a column of numbers from an original copy of a document or dictated document, add the numbers from the original copy or the dictated information to get a total; then add the numbers of what you have just keyed to get a total. The totals should equal. If they do not and the difference between the totals can be divided by nine, you have transposed a number. See the example below:

Original Copy	Keyed Copy
10 boxes	10 boxes
5 tables	5 tables
12 chairs	21 chairs

The total of the items in the original copy is 27; the total of the items in the keyed copy is 36. The difference between the two is 9 which can be divided by 9. You will note that *21 chairs* in the keyed copy should have been *12 chairs*.

A Word Mastery

Directions: Apply what you learned in the English Skills Review. Choose the correct word in the following sentences from those found in the Word Mastery Preview.

1. Your parents made a wonderful _investment_ in your future by helping you with your college tuition.

2. How many people have had the _opportunity_ you had to travel the world?

3. Bob forgot to draw a line after the name of the _payee_ on his check.

4. _Insufficient_ funds were the reason his check was returned.

5. Gloria had made a(n) _overdraft_ on her account which resulted in several bad checks.

6. She decided to have the health club _draft_ her monthly membership fee from her bank.

7. The investments Simon made were not _yielding_ a good return.

8. We encourage our customers to make _deposits_ to their savings accounts as often as possible.

9. Because he started saving early through a(n) _IRA_, he was able to retire much earlier than he planned.

10. Sam decided he would not accept a credit card but only cash or a(n) _cashier's check_ when he sold the antique desk to the buyer.

B Word Usage

Directions: Choose the correct word in each of the following sentences.

1. Next (weak, week) we will have to look at your investment portfolio.

2. Don't you want to (buy, by) the best product for your money?

3. He is a (disinterested, uninterested) party; therefore, he will be fair in his decision.

4. My two children often argue if they think one has (less, lesser, least) candy than the other.

5. (Among, Between) you and me, I think John is going to take the financial manager position.

6. Do you think the evidence is (real, really)?

7. She will, of course, (cease, seize) the opportunity to take center stage again.

8. The students seem very (disinterested, uninterested) in the lesson about grammar.

9. Don't share this secret (among, between) all your classmates!

10. Sarah Jessica seems to be a very (weak, week) math student.

C Spelling

Directions: Choose the correct spelling in each of the following sentences.

1. The president will (beleive, believe) what you say (until, untill) she thinks you are not being honest.

2. It is not (unuseual, unusual) for people to (exceed, excede) the speed limit.

3. When you go (through, though) a very difficult time, you can become bitter or better.

4. As we approached the (nineth, ninth) stop light, I realized we would be late for the meeting.

5. Don't (withold, withhold) any information; even the smallest fact could make a (difference, differance).

6. If you fail to plan, then you are (planing, planning) to fail; therefore, you will not be (successful, successfull).

7. It is best not to (criticise, criticize) others.

8. What was your checkbook (balance, ballance) before you wrote the last check?

9. Many people (mispell, misspell) words, and it could be avoided if they would use a dictionary.

10. It is (acceptable, acceptible) for her name to (precede, preceed) mine on the program.

D Language Skills

Directions: Use proofreaders' marks to make corrections in the following sentences. Write "Correct" by the sentence if no corrections are needed.

1. I couldn't believe I found $20.00 in the hallway.

2. Each of us contributed $.75 toward his meal since it was his birthday.

3. Several years ago on April 12 2008 we took our first cruise to Alaska.

4. On page 32 12 items have been omitted.

5. We usually tip 15% or more if we feel we have received good service.

6. He opened the first account on June 3 2001 when he was only 15 years old.

7. We found 50 cents under the sofa.

8. We had hoped to deposit $100.00 each month in savings.

9. Was the ten percent discount given to everyone?

10. In column 22, 11 names were omitted by mistake.

E Composition

1. Compose and key a paragraph applying the word mastery, word usage, spelling, and language skills you have studied.

2. Compose and key a second paragraph that explains how a wise financial investment now might help you in the future.

3. Compose and key a third paragraph about a special occasion, stating the month, day, and year it occurred and using the correct punctuation for dates. Submit all three paragraphs to your instructor.

F Research

1. Conduct research using the Internet, newspaper, and library or talk with individuals who are actually employed in the banking, financial management, and consumer credit fields to obtain information about the topics listed below. When searching online, go to the U.S. Bureau of Labor Statistics website at **www.bls.gov** and click on the **Publications** tab. Then click on the *Occupational Outlook Handbook* and **Index** links. Click on the first letter of the name of the field. (Example: Click on the letter *B* and scroll down the screen to find information on *banking*.) You can also do an online search of the name of the field/industry followed by the words *career* or *training*. (Example: *banking career* or *banking training*)

   • What are the employment opportunities for office workers in the banking, financial management, and consumer credit fields?

   • What are the advantages and/or disadvantages of employment in these fields?

   • What skills or characteristics are necessary for someone who wants to work in these fields?

   • What are the job titles or positions in these fields?

   • What are the salary ranges for positions in these fields?

   • What additional information did you learn during this research?

2. Compose a document by keying paragraphs that address the questions above. Add a meaningful title. Include your name and the date. Proofread, edit, and revise the paragraphs to correct all grammar and spelling errors. Print the document. Proofread it again and make any final changes before submitting it to your instructor.

Enclosure notations let the reader of the correspondence know what should be included with the correspondence. Review the proper format for enclosure notations as described below.

Enclosure Notations

- Tap ENTER once after the reference initials and key the enclosure notation at the left margin.

- Tap TAB to align the listing of enclosures at 1" if you choose to list the enclosures.

- The word *Enclosure* or *Enclosures* is acceptable without listing the items.

- Using *Enclosures: 5* (or the appropriate number of items enclosed) is also acceptable if you have several items and do not wish to list them.

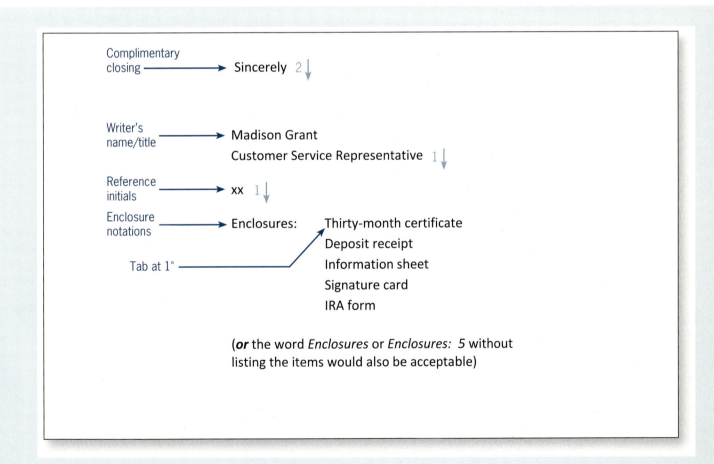

TRANSCRIPTION EXERCISES

1. Transcribe the Word Mastery terms from the Transcription CD.

2. Transcribe the five documents from the Transcription CD following the instructions below and using the current date.

   • Open Document 1 and use the letterhead for San Francisco Bank and Trust. Key this document in modified block letter style with mixed punctuation.

   • Open Document 2 and use the letterhead for Citizens and Southern Savings. Key this document in modified block letter style with open punctuation.

   • Open Document 3 and use the letterhead for Community National Bank. Key this document in modified block letter style with open punctuation.

   • Open Document 4 and use the letterhead for Bank of St. Louis. Key this document in block letter style with open punctuation.

   • Open Document 5 and use the letterhead for Bank of St. Louis. Key this document in block letter style with mixed punctuation.

3. When you have transcribed a document using the file from the Transcription CD, remember to use the **Save As** feature and a distinctive name as the file name for each document.

4. Spell-check, proofread, and submit all five documents to your instructor for approval.

CHAPTER CHECKPOINTS

Place a check mark beside the objectives you can meet after completing this chapter.

_____ I can define, spell, and use the Word Mastery terms in this chapter.

_____ I can use the commonly misused terms from the Word Usage section in this chapter.

_____ I can spell correctly the words in the Spelling section in this chapter.

_____ I can apply the rules for commas presented in the Language Skills section in this chapter.

_____ I can apply the rules for number/figure style presented in the Language Skills section in this chapter.

_____ I can transcribe documents containing enclosure notations and proofread carefully.

✳ Evaluation Form

Access the Evaluation Form from your Transcription CD. Complete it and submit it with your work. You may choose to either print the form and complete it or complete the form electronically.

IMPORTANT NOTE: Check with your instructor regarding the testing procedures for Part 1 (Chapters 1–6).

PART 2
Intermediate Machine Transcription

Why did you decide to do this type of work?

"I decided to do this type of work because it is interesting to me."

Who inspired you to consider working in transcription?

"I inspired myself because I like to type."

Where did you learn how to transcribe?

"I learned how to transcribe at one of my previous clerical jobs."

When did you first begin transcribing?

"I began in 1995 at Truman Arnold Co."

How did you educationally prepare for your current position?

"I took typing in high school and from there I found that on-the-job training was helpful, but the Office Career Course was what really got me prepared educationally. In the course, I used MACHINE TRANSCRIPTION AND DICTATION, Fifth Edition, by Mitsy Ballentine."

On-the-job training is good experience, but you definitely want to take a transcription course . . . because this type of learning is invaluable.

What do you enjoy the most and the least about transcribing?

"What I like the most is the transcription work I do for the Police Department; it is interesting because it is always something different. The thing I like the least is when people talk too fast or too low and you have to rewind more than once to be able to understand the dictation."

What advice would you give a student regarding transcription?

"On-the-job training is good experience, but you definitely want to take a transcription course in college because this type of learning is invaluable. You need to have or learn to have patience as well."

LEARNING OBJECTIVES

After completing all the learning activities in this chapter, you will be able to:

- Define, spell, and use the Word Mastery terms.

- Use commonly misused words appropriately.

- Use correct spelling for commonly misspelled words.

- Apply the rules for dashes, questions marks, and quotation marks presented in this chapter.

- Apply the rules for number/ figure style presented in this chapter.

- Apply proofreading and transcription skills.

- Transcribe documents containing copy notations.

Chapter 7

INSURANCE

The insurance field includes many types of insurance such as life, health, dental, cancer, automobile, and homeowners. There are also many different positions within the insurance field. They include insurance agents, underwriters, adjusters, and investigators. A high school education is sufficient to qualify for some positions, but an associate's or a bachelor's degree is preferred. Many positions also require special certification or licensing.

Word Mastery Preview

Directions: Review the list of Word Mastery terms that will be used in the documents you will be transcribing. Learn the definition for each word and how to spell it correctly.

life insurance	*Definition:*	insurance that provides payments on the death of the policy holder
	Example:	J. D. purchased life insurance from an insurance company.
long-term care insurance	*Definition:*	insurance that provides care for those who require custodial care
	Example:	Most people do not realize the value of long-term care insurance.
long-term disability insurance	*Definition:*	insurance that protects a portion of your income if you become disabled while on the job
	Example:	Because Anne had long-term disability insurance, she still received income while she was recovering from her injury.
exclusions	*Definition:*	items not covered under the insurance policy
	Example:	There were numerous exclusions listed in the policy that Jonathan did not read.
limitations	*Definition:*	maximum amounts covered under an insurance policy
	Example:	The limitations were listed on page 15 of the insurance policy.
policies	*Definition:*	insurance documents
	Example:	One should keep insurance policies in a safe deposit box.
dependents	*Definition:*	an individual's spouse or young children
	Example:	Ruth and Don's dependents were their two daughters.

eligible

Definition: legally qualified to be covered under an insurance plan

Example: All employees must work six months with the company before they will be eligible for insurance.

coverage

Definition: protection against risk provided by a policy

Example: Do you think you have enough coverage on your home?

COBRA

Definition: abbreviation for Consolidated Omnibus Budget Reconciliation Act; continued insurance coverage that may be obtained if a person loses his or her current health insurance from the employer

Example: Because he lost his job, he was eligible for COBRA coverage.

reimbursement

Definition: the act of repayment for medical expenses

Example: Stephen hopes to receive his reimbursement quickly.

deductible

Definition: the amount of covered medical expenses you must pay annually before the insurance company pays any benefits

Example: Harold exceeded his $200 deductible during his first month of coverage.

out-of-pocket

Definition: a nonreimbursable expense paid for medical services

Example: My insurance policy pays 80 percent of my medical expenses; the remaining 20 percent are out-of-pocket expenses.

lifetime maximum benefit

Definition: the maximum amount the insurance company will pay for each person in his/her lifetime

Example: Unfortunately, Robert exceeded his lifetime maximum benefit because of major illnesses during his life.

B Word Usage

Directions: Learn to spell and define these confusing words, which may occur within the documents you will be transcribing.

accede	(verb) to agree; to give in
exceed	(verb) go beyond
all together	(pronoun and adverb) a group together
altogether	(adverb) entirely
any way	(adjective and noun) by any manner
anyway	(adverb) in any case
could have	(verb) use *have* with this phrase, not the word *of*
should have	(verb) use *have* with this phrase, not the word *of*
would have	(verb) use *have* with this phrase, not the word *of*
eligible	(adjective) qualified; entitled
illegible	(adjective) impossible to read
ensure	(verb) to guarantee or to make sure
insure	(verb) to cover or to underwrite
one	(noun) a single unit, person, or thing
won	(verb) to achieve victory

C Spelling

Directions: Learn to spell these common words.

advisable	existence	maintenance
argument	familiar	naturally
before	government	persuade
collectible	indispensable	surprise
dilemma	length	vehicle

D Language Skills

Directions: Enhance your language skills by reviewing basic grammar, punctuation, capitalization, number/figure style, abbreviation style, and word division rules. Study the rules and examples below.

Rule: Use the dash before words that summarize the preceding part of the sentence.

Examples:
- Peaches, bananas, and apples—these are my favorite fruits.
- Ann, Jackie, Phyllis, Janice, Billy, Betty, and Cathy—the women in my club are so unique and different.

Rule: Use a question mark after a direct question. Do not use a question mark after indirect questions or polite requests.

Examples:
- Would you like to go to the movies tonight? (direct question)
- She asked if she could attend the meeting today. (indirect question)
- May I see you in my office immediately after class. (polite request)

Rule: Use quotation marks to enclose direct quotations. (Direct quotations are the exact words that someone has said or written.) Place the period or comma inside the closing quotation marks. The first word of a direct quote always begins with a capital letter. Do not use quotation marks to enclose indirect quotations. (Indirect quotations are not the exact words that someone has said or written.)

Examples:
- Heather said, "Our family will not be attending the wedding."
- Heather said that her family would not be attending the wedding.
- "We cannot afford to buy a larger home," her husband stated.
- Her husband stated that they could not afford to buy a larger home.

Rule: Spell out numbers up to and including ten; use figures for numbers over ten.

Examples:
- There were four birds sitting on the branch of the tree.
- Although all the class could not go out to eat together, 13 of the students ate lunch in the cafeteria.

Rule: Spell out time used with *o'clock*. Use figures for time with the abbreviations *a.m.* and *p.m.*

Examples:
- We will not have our meeting until two o'clock.
- Your flight is at 8:15 a.m.

Proofreading
Tips

- When proofreading material, check your punctuation marks very carefully. You would be surprised how much difference punctuation can make in the meaning of a sentence. Look at the examples below:

The business owner stated, "The customer is always right."

"The business owner," stated the customer, "is always right."

- Note in the two examples above that both sentences include the exact same words; however, the way each sentence has been punctuated makes a major difference. In the first example, the business owner is speaking and states that the customer is always right. In the second example, the customer is speaking and states that the business owner is always right.

ENGLISH SKILLS EXERCISES

A Word Mastery

Directions: Apply what you learned in the English Skills Review. Choose the correct word in the following sentences from those found in the Word Mastery Preview.

1. Mr. Jordan could not find his _____ policy.

2. Because she had three children, she listed all three as her _____.

3. Since she had lost her job and was no longer covered under her company's insurance, she decided to obtain insurance under _____.

4. Shakeeta had met her _____; therefore, her insurance company would pay the rest of her doctor's bill.

5. Many people think they will never use enough insurance to reach their _____.

6. Lisa was not aware that she may need _____ in order to provide for her care when she is older.

7. Many companies offer their employees _____ that will provide a portion of their income should they become disabled while working.

8. You should keep important papers such as your life insurance _____ in a convenient, secure location.

9. Before an insurance company will pay benefits, an individual will have to pay some _____ expenses.

10. If there are any _____ in an insurance policy, their maximum amounts will be indicated in the policy.

B Word Usage

Directions: Choose the correct word in each of the following sentences.

1. She tried (anyway, any way) she could to get insurance for her family.

2. Agnes (one, won) her lawsuit against the insurance company.

3. Because he had a broken finger, the note he wrote was (eligible, illegible).

4. The chorus traveled (all together, altogether) on the school bus.

5. Because of his preexisting conditions, the company would not (ensure, insure) him for medical coverage.

6. Robert (could of, could have) been insured if he had accepted the company's benefit package.

7. Did he (accede, exceed) the expectations you had?

8. You were (all together, altogether) wrong in the decision you made regarding this request.

9. Although his parents had warned him not to drive their car, he did so (anyway, any way).

10. Don't you think he should be (eligible, illegible) to participate in the contest next week?

C Spelling

Directions: Choose the correct spelling in each of the following sentences.

1. Jason's (vehicle, vehical) was involved in the automobile accident.

2. Although it was not (advisable, advisible) for her, she decided to get involved in her friend's (argument, arguement) with her boyfriend.

3. (Naturally, Naturelly), you should be very (familar, familiar) with the case (befor, before) you decide whether you are going to represent the client.

4. Barbie dolls are (collectible, collectable) toys that people have saved for decades.

5. Before Joan was able to (persuade, persuede) her employer to fire Melanie, Melanie decided to take a position with the federal (goverment, government).

6. Because the (lenght, length) of the dress was too short, Mary had to choose another outfit to wear to the office.

7. It was a difficult (delimma, dilemma) for Joseph when he had to tell his best friend that his insurance policy did not cover the damage.

8. Although the party was to be a (serprise, surprise), Logan found out about it two hours before the event.

9. Zelda was not aware of the (existance, existence) of several valuable coins until she opened the safe deposit box.

10. (Maintainance, Maintenance) on your (vehicle, vehical) is important to keep it in safe condition.

D Language Skills

Directions: Use proofreaders' marks to make corrections in the following sentences. Write "Correct" by the sentence if no corrections are needed.

1. Which of the ten items did you not receive?

2. We will not be late for the 4 o'clock funeral.

3. Toys, games, and clothes these are the items that many children receive for their birthdays.

4. May we have your answer as soon as possible.

5. Charlene said, "My office needs to be repainted soon".

6. We expected twelve people to attend the insurance meeting.

7. Don't begin the meeting until nine a.m. or you won't have many present.

8. Life, health, automobile, home, disability these are the different types of insurance he sells.

9. Doris said, my sister's insurance will probably be cancelled if she doesn't pay her premiums.

10. Fred said, "that he hoped he could locate his insurance policy in his safe deposit box at the bank."

E Composition

1. Compose and key a paragraph applying the word mastery, word usage, spelling, and language skills you have studied.

2. Compose and key a second paragraph about some items a homeowner's insurance policy might exclude, such as trampolines.

3. Compose and key a third paragraph that includes a list of questions you might want to ask about an insurance policy you are going to purchase. Submit all three paragraphs to your instructor.

F Research

1. Conduct research using the Internet, newspaper, and library or talk with individuals who are actually employed in the insurance field to obtain information about the topics listed below. When searching online, go to the U.S. Bureau of Labor Statistics website at **www.bls.gov** and click on the **Publications** tab. Then click on the ***Occupational Outlook Handbook*** and **Index** links. Click on the first letter of the name of the field. (Example: Click on the letter *I* and scroll down the screen to find information on *insurance*.) You can also do an online search of the name of the field/industry followed by the words *career* or *training*. (Example: *insurance career* or *insurance training*)

   - What are the employment opportunities for office workers in the insurance field?

   - What are the advantages and/or disadvantages of employment in this field?

   - What skills or characteristics are necessary for someone who wants to work in this field?

   - What are the job titles or positions in this field?

   - What are the salary ranges for positions in this field?

   - What additional information did you learn during this research?

2. Compose a document by keying paragraphs that address the questions above. Add a meaningful title. Include your name and the date. Proofread, edit, and revise the paragraphs to correct all grammar and spelling errors. Print the document. Proofread it again and make any final changes before submitting it to your instructor.

TRANSCRIPTION PREVIEW

If you want a copy of the correspondence sent to an individual, you need to denote it at the bottom of the letter with a copy notation. Review the proper format for copy notations as described below and on the next page.

Copy Notation

- Tap ENTER once after the reference initials or the Enclosure notation (if used).

- Key a lowercase *c* at the left margin. Then tap TAB to align the name(s) at 0.5″. Key the name of the person to whom the copy of the correspondence is being sent.

- If more than one person is to receive a copy, denote the name or names of those individuals. Be sure to align their names and remove the extra space between lines.

- Send the original correspondence to the name of the person in the letter address.

- Place a check mark by the name or highlight the name of the person to whom the copy is to be sent. Then send that "copy" to the individual.

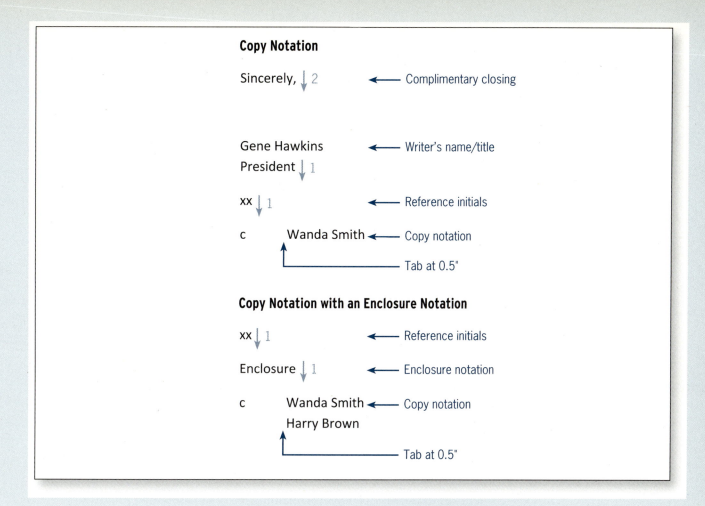

Copy Notation

Sincerely, ↓ 2 ←— Complimentary closing

Gene Hawkins ←— Writer's name/title
President ↓ 1

xx ↓ 1 ←— Reference initials

c   Wanda Smith ←— Copy notation

⎣————————— Tab at 0.5"

Copy Notation with an Enclosure Notation

xx ↓ 1 ←— Reference initials

Enclosure ↓ 1 ←— Enclosure notation

c   Wanda Smith ←— Copy notation
      Harry Brown

⎣————————— Tab at 0.5"

TRANSCRIPTION EXERCISES

1. Transcribe the Word Mastery terms from the Transcription CD.

2. Transcribe the five documents from the Transcription CD following the instructions below and using the current date.

   - Open Document 1 and use the letterhead for Oklahoma State Insurance Company. Key this document in block letter style with open punctuation.

   - Open Document 2 and use the letterhead for Hinson Insurance Agency. Key this document in modified block letter style with open punctuation.

   - Open Document 3 and use the letterhead for Homeowner's Insurance Company of America. Key this document in block letter style with open punctuation.

   - Open Document 4 and use the letterhead for Insurance of New York. Key this document in the memorandum format.

   - Open Document 5 and use the letterhead for Oklahoma State Insurance Company. Key this document in modified block letter style with mixed punctuation.

3. When you have transcribed a document using the file from the Transcription CD, remember to use the **Save As** feature and a distinctive name as the file name for each document.

4. Spell-check, proofread, and submit all five documents to your instructor for approval.

CHAPTER CHECKPOINTS

Place a check mark beside the objectives you can meet after completing this chapter.

_____ I can define, spell, and use the Word Mastery terms in this chapter.

_____ I can use the commonly misused terms from the Word Usage section in this chapter.

_____ I can spell correctly the words in the Spelling section in this chapter.

_____ I can apply the rules for dashes, question marks, and quotation marks presented in the Language Skills section in this chapter.

_____ I can apply the rules for number/figure style presented in the Language Skills section in this chapter.

_____ I can transcribe documents containing copy notations and proofread carefully.

Evaluation Form

Access the Evaluation Form from your Transcription CD. Complete it and submit it with your work. You may choose to either print the form and complete it or complete the form electronically.

©RAGMA IMAGES, 2010/Used under license from Shutterstock.com

Chapter 8

ENGINEERING, INDUSTRIAL, AND MANUFACTURING

Branches in the engineering field include electrical, mechanical, civil, industrial, chemical, and architectural engineering. To be an engineer, you need a college degree.

There are several different types of industrial and manufacturing plants that produce a finished product from raw materials. For example, a manufacturing plant might produce men's shirts from cotton.

A college degree is required for executive positions in all of these fields. Many companies also prefer a graduate degree in either field and/or an MBA (master's degree in business administration). These fields require you to have a strong knowledge of computer training. If you have an analytical mind and enjoy seeing a project through to its completion, these fields would be of interest to you.

LEARNING OBJECTIVES

After completing all the learning activities in this chapter, you will be able to:

- Define, spell, and use the Word Mastery terms.

- Use commonly misused words appropriately.

- Use correct spelling for commonly misspelled words.

- Apply the rules for colons, dashes, exclamation points, and semicolons presented in this chapter.

- Apply the rules for state and territory abbreviations presented in this chapter.

- Apply proofreading and transcription skills.

ENGLISH SKILLS REVIEW

 A **Word Mastery Preview**

Directions: Review the list of Word Mastery terms that will be used in the documents you will be transcribing. Learn the definition for each word and how to spell it correctly.

generators	*Definition:*	electrical device used to convert mechanical energy to electrical energy
	Example:	An alternator on a car is a type of generator.
reactor	*Definition:*	a device whose primary purpose is to introduce reactance into a circuit
	Example:	Reactors are very large coils used in power plants.
capacitor	*Definition:*	a device for accumulating and holding a charge of electricity
	Example:	The capacitor in your television needs to be replaced.
resistor	*Definition:*	a device used to introduce resistance into an electric circuit
	Example:	They added a resistor to the stereo speaker to balance the current.
transformer	*Definition:*	an electrical device, which by electromagnetic induction, transfers electrical energy from one or more circuits to another set of circuits
	Example:	The transformer for the electricity to their home was struck by lightning.
trip	*Definition:*	to shut down a circuit
	Example:	When he put a paper clip into the wall receptacle, it tripped the breaker.
voltage	*Definition:*	electromotive force or potential difference expressed in volts
	Example:	High-voltage warning signs were placed on the electric wiring.

fiber optics	*Definition:*	a technique of electronic communication through laser light waves; uses flexible threadlike fiberglass or plastic instead of traditional copper wires
	Example:	Fiber optics are used extensively in telecommunications.
robotics	*Definition:*	technology dealing with the design, construction, and operation of robots in automation
	Example:	The use of robotics has increased our production.
CAD/CAM	*Definition:*	the abbreviation for Computer Aided Design/Computer Aided Manufacturing; computer technology used in designing and manufacturing
	Example:	Jake plans to enroll in the CAD/CAM program at his college next spring.
raw materials	*Definition:*	unprocessed goods
	Example:	Raw materials were gathered from various sources to make the completed product.
backlog	*Definition:*	an accumulation of stock or work
	Example:	Because of the backlog, many people will have to work overtime to complete the work.
batches	*Definition:*	a quantity of material or number of things of the same kind made or handled at one time or considered as one group
	Example:	The checks were processed in batches in the operation center of the bank.

B Word Usage

Directions: Learn to spell and define these confusing words, which may occur within the documents you will be transcribing.

alternate	(noun or verb) a substitute; to change repeatedly from one to another
alternative	(noun or adjective) a choice between or among things or actions; other
cell	(noun) compartment; small chamber
sell	(verb) to put up for sale

Word Usage (*continued*)

different from	(adjective) shows that one thing is unlike something else
different than	*do not use; incorrect expression*

shear	(verb) to cut or wrench
sheer	(adjective or adverb) thin; vertically

straight	(adjective or adverb) honest; not crooked
strait	(noun) narrow waterway

weald	(noun) a rural area
wheeled	(adjective) having wheels
wield	(verb) to use or to apply

weld	(verb) to join metal by melting its edges
welled	(verb) pouring forth

 Spelling

Directions: Learn to spell these common words.

acreage	**disastrous**	**maneuver**
annually	**equipped**	**safety**
apparent	**fluorescent**	**underrate**
competition	**gauge**	**upholstery**
consensus	**interruption**	**usable**

 Language Skills

Directions: Enhance your language skills by reviewing basic grammar, punctuation, capitalization, number/figure style, abbreviation style, and word division rules. Study the rules and examples below.

Rule:	Use a colon to introduce a listing that is not immediately preceded by a preposition or a verb. *The following, as follows, such as these,* and *thus* are anticipatory expressions that often precede a listing.
Examples:	• The house has attractive features: a fireplace, large family room, and three full baths.
	• I need to see the following people: Jackson Brooks, Meredith Henderson, and Tammy Green.
	• Gloria likes to eat hamburgers, pizza, and hot dogs.
	• The blouse comes in beige, white, or black.

Rule: Use a dash instead of a comma when emphasizing a repeated thought or statement.

Examples:
- You will need to study–study daily–if you want to be successful in this course.

- When you learn–truly learn–your grammar rules, you will not be as stressed when you have to apply those rules to sentences.

Rule: Use an exclamation point at the end of a thought expressing strong emotion or a command.

Examples:
- Wow! I won a million dollars!

- Don't make me tell you again to clean up your room!

Rule: Use a semicolon between items in a listing if any of the items already contain commas.

Examples:
- My children's birthdates are April 21, 2004; June 8, 2005; and September 24, 1996.

- Jose has visited Washington, D.C.; Honolulu, Hawaii; and Juneau, Alaska.

Rule: State names are usually spelled out; however, you should use the two-letter state abbreviations for state names when used as part of an inside address of a letter or on the envelope.

Examples:
- I lived in Jackson, Mississippi, before moving to Greenville, Mississippi.

- Send the letter to Mr. John Smith, 14 South Hampton Lane, Greenville, MS 38701-1234.

Proofreading Tips

- Check your facts correctly. Don't assume that the originator who dictated the information or the writer who wrote the information has listed all the information correctly. Can you find the errors in the following paragraph?

I have visited one state capital every year for the past five years. The state capitals I have visited are Atlanta, Georgia; Charleston, South Carolina; Charlotte, North Carolina; and Tallahassee, Florida.

- There are several errors. Charleston and Charlotte are not the capitals of the states mentioned. Columbia is the state capital of South Carolina, and Raleigh is the state capital of North Carolina. The originator stated he/she had visited a state capital every year for the past five years; however, only four cities, not five, are mentioned.

ENGLISH SKILLS EXERCISES

A Word Mastery

Directions: Apply what you learned in the English Skills Review. Choose the correct word in the following sentences from those found in the Word Mastery Preview.

1. The _____ of the electricity was clearly indicated.

2. Through her training in _____, she was able to use the computer to assist her with her design.

3. If we want to go home by 5 p.m. and not work overtime, we will need to complete all the _____.

4. Ramon prepared several _____ of cookies for the party.

5. The company had too many _____ that needed to be processed into the final product.

6. Since the company has installed _____, they have increased their production.

7. Because the lightning had damaged the _____ that was connected to the store, there was no electricity for days.

8. The _____ at the plant were down which means all production was halted due to no electrical energy.

9. Power plants have _____ that are large coils used to introduce reactance into a circuit.

10. Don't _____ the breaker by putting anything into the wall receptacle.

B Word Usage

Directions: Choose the correct word in each of the following sentences.

1. The (alternate, alternative) route for the trucks was closed due to road construction.

2. After he removed the fluid from the (cell, sell) that contained the hazardous material, he was able to clean it thoroughly.

3. Your answers are totally (different than, different from) my answers.

4. Don't (weald, wheeled, wield) that light saber in the house or you could break something.

5. The fabric was too (shear, sheer) to use for the draperies.

6. When my daughter made the honor roll, my eyes (weld, welled) up with tears.

7. Why don't you use a (straight, strait) line to connect the two points?

8. I hope we will be able to (cell, sell) the items even though they are used.

9. My husband will (weld, welled) the two pieces together so no one will ever know the iron table was broken.

10. After he had started to (shear, sheer) the material, Allen realized he had made an error in the measurements.

C Spelling

Directions: Choose the correct spelling in each of the following sentences.

1. The (upholestary, upholstery) fabric was not (useable, usable) for the new office chairs.

2. Based on the (disasterous, disastrous) outcome, it was (apparant, apparent) to everyone that the choice the company made was not a wise decision.

3. Don't (underate, underrate) her ability to (manuver, maneuver) the truck as well as a man.

4. The general (concensus, consensus) was to hold the (competetion, competition) at the local college.

5. (Annualy, Annually) we evaluate our objectives so we know whether we are meeting the goals of the company.

6. Because there is so much (acerage, acreage), Joe knew he was not going to be able care for his family farm alone.

7. The service worker checked every (gage, gauge) on the heating unit carefully to determine why it was not working correctly.

8. The flickering of the (fluorescent, fluoresent) lighting caused an (interuption, interruption) in business.

9. There are many guidelines in place to make sure (safety, safty) is not compromised in our plant.

10. Although we thought we were (equipt, equipped) to handle the influx of business, we could not keep up with the demand.

D Language Skills

Directions: Use proofreaders' marks to make corrections in the following sentences. Write "Correct" by the sentence if no corrections are needed.

1. If you plan to graduate by May, you will need to take the following courses this semester Document Production OST 210 Machine Transcription OST 121 and Introduction to Computers CPT 101.

2. We often pick up a quick lunch at McDonalds, Taco Bell, or Burger King.

3. Gee whiz I thought I lost my car keys.

4. We often quite often think of our own needs rather than the needs of others.

5. Our company will be represented at the meeting by Leslie Couric director Matt Dillon marketing manager and Daniel Scott supervisor.

6. You must correct that situation immediately and I mean immediately before we have a voltage problem.

7. If you prepare really prepare for your presentation for the robotics convention, you will be more confident.

8. Topics such as these will be offered at the seminar CAD/CAM, robotics, and fiber optics.

9. He has been transferred three times from the following locations Greenville South Carolina Charleston West Virginia and Charlotte North Carolina.

10. On the brown envelope, key the following address Mrs. Sallie Foster, 1435 Eastside Drive, Noblesville, Indiana 46060-2345.

E Composition

1. Compose and key a paragraph applying the word mastery, word usage, spelling, and language skills you have studied.

2. Compose and key a second paragraph about the occurrence of backlog in an office environment.

3. Compose and key a third paragraph that lists various ways robotics are being used today. Submit all three paragraphs to your instructor.

F Research

1. Conduct research using the Internet, newspaper, and library or talk with individuals who are actually employed in the engineering, industrial, and manufacturing fields to obtain information about the topics listed below. When searching online, go to the U.S. Bureau of Labor Statistics website at **www.bls.gov** and click on the **Publications** tab. Then click on the ***Occupational Outlook Handbook*** and **Index** links. Click on the first letter of the name of the field. (Example: Click on the letter *E* and scroll down the screen to find information on *engineering*.) You can also do an online search of the name of the field/industry followed by the words *career* or *training*. (Example: *engineering career* or *engineering training*)

- What are the employment opportunities for office workers in the engineering, industrial, or manufacturing fields?

- What are the advantages and/or disadvantages of employment in these fields?

- What skills or characteristics are necessary for someone who wants to work in these fields?

- What are the job titles or positions in these fields?

- What are the salary ranges for positions in these fields?

- What additional information did you learn during this research?

2. Compose a document by keying paragraphs that address the questions above. Add a meaningful title. Include your name and the date. Proofread, edit, and revise the paragraphs to correct all grammar and spelling errors. Print the document. Proofread it again and make any final changes before submitting it to your instructor.

TRANSCRIPTION PREVIEW

You need to be familiar with the spelling of state names and their two-letter abbreviations. The two-letter state and territory abbreviations shown below are most commonly used in addresses in letters and on envelopes.

Two-Letter State and Territory Abbreviations

Alabama, AL	Kentucky, KY	Oklahoma, OK
Alaska, AK	Louisiana, LA	Oregon, OR
Arizona, AZ	Maine, ME	Pennsylvania, PA
Arkansas, AR	Maryland, MD	Puerto Rico, PR
California, CA	Massachusetts, MA	Rhode Island, RI
Colorado, CO	Michigan, MI	South Carolina, SC
Connecticut, CT	Minnesota, MN	South Dakota, SD
Delaware, DE	Mississippi, MS	Tennessee, TN
District of	Missouri, MO	Texas, TX
Columbia, DC	Montana, MT	Utah, UT
Florida, FL	Nebraska, NE	Vermont, VT
Georgia, GA	Nevada, NV	Virgin Islands, VI
Guam, GU	New Hampshire, NH	Virginia, VA
Hawaii, HI	New Jersey, NJ	Washington, WA
Idaho, ID	New Mexico, NM	West Virginia, WV
Illinois, IL	New York, NY	Wisconsin, WI
Indiana, IN	North Carolina, NC	Wyoming, WY
Iowa, IA	North Dakota, ND	
Kansas, KS	Ohio, OH	

1. Transcribe the Word Mastery terms from the Transcription CD.

2. Transcribe the five documents from the Transcription CD as described below. Key the documents in memorandum format and use the current date.

   - Open Document 1 and use the letterhead for Acme Electrical Engineering.

   - Open Document 2 and use the letterhead for Jackson Engineering, Inc.

   - Open Document 3 and use the letterhead for Southwestern Manufacturing.

   - Open Document 4 and use the letterhead for Minnesota Manufacturing.

   - Open Document 5 and use the letterhead for Minnesota Manufacturing.

3. When you have transcribed a document using the file from the Transcription CD, remember to use the **Save As** feature and a distinctive name as the file name for each document.

4. Spell-check, proofread, and submit all five documents to your instructor for approval.

CHAPTER CHECKPOINTS

Place a check mark beside the objectives you can meet after completing this chapter.

_____ I can define, spell, and use the Word Mastery terms in this chapter.

_____ I can use the commonly misused terms from the Word Usage section in this chapter.

_____ I can spell correctly the words in the Spelling section in this chapter.

_____ I can apply the rules for colons, dashes, exclamation points, and semicolons presented in the Language Skills section in this chapter.

_____ I can apply the rules for state and territory abbreviations presented in the Language Skills section in this chapter.

✳ Evaluation Form

Access the Evaluation Form from your Transcription CD. Complete it and submit it with your work. You may choose to either print the form and complete it or complete the form electronically.

©Yuri Arcurs/Shutterstock.com

Chapter 9

ENTERTAINMENT, FOOD, AND RESTAURANT SERVICES

More and more people are dining out today and spending more money on various types of entertainment. An individual needs strong interpersonal skills and a clear perception of customer needs to be successful in the entertainment, food, and restaurant services industries. Some management areas in these industries require an associate's or a bachelor's degree, although some food service managers may have only a high school diploma.

ENGLISH SKILLS REVIEW

 A **Word Mastery Preview**

Directions: Review the list of Word Mastery terms that will be used in the documents you will be transcribing. Learn the definition for each word and how to spell it correctly.

dignitaries	*Definition:*	people who hold a high rank or office
	Example:	During the election, we saw many dignitaries shaking hands with voters.

quote	*Definition:*	to state a price
	Example:	When you quote the exact amount for catering my daughter's wedding, I will sign the contract.

buffet	*Definition:*	a meal laid out on a table so that guests may serve themselves
	Example:	Many restaurants offer a Sunday buffet.

nonrefundable	*Definition:*	no repayment
	Example:	Because we were told there was a nonrefundable charge, we decided not to purchase the item.

catering	*Definition:*	the act of providing food service
	Example:	After she worked for a restaurant, Audrey decided to open her own catering service.

deterioration	*Definition:*	a decline in quality, function, or condition
	Example:	The deterioration of the house occurred over the years.

entrée	*Definition:*	the main course of a meal
	Example:	The entrée was served after the dinner salad had been removed from the table.

filet mignon	*Definition:*	a small, tender round of steak cut from the thick end of a beef tenderloin
	Example:	Mike always orders filet mignon.

cordon bleu	*Definition:*	a dish cooked with ham and cheese
	Example:	Chicken cordon bleu is the specialty of the house.

maitre d'	*Definition:*	the head waiter
	Example:	Our maitre d' directed us to our table.

B Word Usage

Directions: Learn to spell and define these confusing words, which may occur within the documents you will be transcribing.

ail	(verb) to be ill
ale	(noun) beverage

awesome	(adjective) full of awe; splendid
awful	(adjective) really bad

beat	(verb) to hit
beet	(noun) an edible red root

bite	(noun or verb) a mouthful; to chew
byte	(noun) eight bits (computer term)

chef	(noun) a trained cook
chief	(noun or adjective) a leader or the person in charge; most important

maise	(noun) corn
maze	(noun) a puzzle

pair	(noun) two of something; a couple
pare	(verb) to cut down
pear	(noun) a fruit

C Spelling

Directions: Learn to spell these common words.

amateur	hygiene	pleasant
committee	invitation	potatoes
fiery	miniature	temperature
grateful	occasion	tongue
hors d'oeuvres	perseverance	vegetarian

D Language Skills

Directions: Enhance your language skills by reviewing basic grammar, punctuation, capitalization, number/figure style, abbreviation style, and word division rules. Study the rules and examples below.

Rule: Use parentheses to enclose figures or letters that mark a series of enumerated elements within a sentence.

Examples:
- The new business on the agenda will cover the following: (1) the building proposal, (2) the fund-raising program, and (3) the dues increase.

- There are three sections in his report as follows: (a) the introduction, (b) the body, and (c) the conclusion.

Rule: Capitalize the names of individuals, buildings, organizations, religious groups, nationalities, and races.

Examples:
- Bill Clinton, a Democrat from Arkansas, was President of the United States and lived in the White House.

- After the First Baptist Church's Reception Hall flooded, several African Americans who attended the Second Baptist Church offered the Mary Burnside Fellowship Hall to the young couple for their wedding reception.

Rule: Capitalize professional titles when they immediately precede individual names. Do not capitalize titles following names except in an address or signature line. When referring to the President of the United States, the word *President* is always capitalized whether or not a name follows it.

Examples:
- Marvin Coker, dean of the college, will speak with Mayor Jesse Jordan.

- Professor Brown had been a professor at Columbia College prior to coming to Winston University.

- The President will address the nation tonight regarding the oil spill disaster.

Rule: Capitalize days of the week, months of the year, and holidays.

Examples: • We celebrate Thanksgiving Day on Thursday, November 22, this year.

• What date in January is Martin Luther King Jr. Day?

ENGLISH SKILLS EXERCISES

A Word Mastery

Directions: Apply what you learned in the English Skills Review. Choose the correct word in the following sentences from those found in the Word Mastery Preview.

1. There were many _____ at the political fund-raising event.

2. She was told that all purchases were final, and all of the items were

    _____.

3. _____ of the fabric occurred because of the damage from the sun and heat.

4. What _____ did you choose to eat at the restaurant?

5. My son was hired as the _____ at the country club.

6. One of the most expensive cuts of beef is the _____.

7. When I was planning my daughter's reception, I was wise to get a(n) _____ on the cost of the caterer.

8. Instead of being served individually by the wait staff, everyone was asked to serve themselves from the _____.

9. Before you consider going into the _____ business, be sure you have considered the costs involved in starting a food service.

10. Chicken _____ is an elegant dish to serve for a banquet.

B Word Usage

Directions: Choose the correct word in each of the following sentences.

1. After the (chef, chief) decided on the menu, he instructed the rest of the staff as to their duties in preparing the dinner.

2. Although Agnes was proud that her daughter prepared the meal, the gravy she made was so (awesome, awful) that no one would eat it.

3. We often think of (maise, maze) when we think of Thanksgiving.

4. (Ail, Ale) was served at the celebration, but no one liked the taste.

5. During the fall many schools have a corn (maise, maze) set up for people to enter and try to determine how to find their way to the exit.

Word Usage (*continued*)

6. The (beat, beet) of the drum was so loud that no one could hear the announcer.

7. Take a small (bite, byte) of the apple so you won't choke.

8. His sermon was so (awesome, awful) that people talked about how inspiring it was for weeks.

9. The (chef, chief) reason we are here is to discuss a solution to our problem.

10. My grandchild would rather have a (pair, pare, pear) than an apple or a banana to eat.

C Spelling

Directions: Choose the correct spelling in each of the following sentences.

1. Mary Louise was so (greatful, grateful) to receive the (invitation, invitetion) to the dance.

2. A (committe, committee) will be selected next week to judge the (amateur, amature) cooking contest.

3. The salsa was so (firey, fiery) that his (tong, tongue) felt like he had burned it.

4. Because Pearl was a (vegetarian, vegeterian), we could not have hamburgers for lunch.

5. If you cook the (potatoes, potatos) too long, they will become very soft.

6. What (temperature, temperture) should I cook the roast?

7. (Hygene, Hygiene) is very important in a kitchen when you are preparing food.

8. His (perseverance, perseverence) made the entire evening so (pleasant, pleasent) for everyone.

9. Since the (ocassion, occasion) was so close to the dinner hour, only (hors d' overs, hors d'oeuvers) were served instead of a full meal.

10. Everyone loved the (minature, miniature) desserts that were served.

D Language Skills

Directions: Use proofreaders' marks to make corrections in the following sentences. Write "Correct" by the sentence if no corrections are needed.

1. We plan to visit the Lincoln Memorial when we visit Washington.

2. Why don't you ask Jacob Lowry, County Treasurer, where the money was spent?

3. Did you see Libby Nelson, Dean of Women, about this issue?

4. We won't be able to visit you on mother's day this year.

5. Let me list the three reasons we didn't hire you: you were late for the interview, your resume was not complete, and you were not dressed appropriately for our type of business.

6. The american cancer society is one charity many people support.

7. Angela McDonald, President of our organization, will be the guest speaker.

8. Why don't we plan on eating the easter buffet at the club.

9. Please remember the following procedures: 1. Prepare the dish, 2. Garnish the dish, and present the dish.

10. The republican and democratic parties will hold their national conventions next year.

E Composition

1. Compose and key a paragraph applying the word mastery, word usage, spelling, and language skills you have studied.

2. Compose and key a second paragraph about the landmarks or tourist sites in the city or state where you live.

3. Compose and key a third paragraph that lists the food items you enjoy the most at your favorite restaurant. Be sure to use the rules regarding enumeration that you have learned in this chapter. Submit all three paragraphs to your instructor.

F Research

1. Conduct research using the Internet, newspaper, and library or talk with individuals who are actually employed in the entertainment, food, and restaurant services fields to obtain information about the topics listed below. When searching online, go to the U.S. Bureau of Labor Statistics website at **www.bls.gov** and click on the **Publications** tab. Then click on the *Occupational Outlook Handbook* and **Index** links. Click on the first letter of the name of the field. (Example: Click on the letter *E* and scroll down the screen to find information on *entertainment*.) You can also do an online search of the name of the field/industry followed by the words *career* or *training*. (Example: *entertainment career* or *entertainment training*)

   - What are the employment opportunities for office workers in the entertainment, food, or restaurant services fields?

   - What are the advantages and/or disadvantages of employment in these fields?

   - What skills or characteristics are necessary for someone who wants to work in these fields?

   - What are the job titles or positions in these fields?

   - What are the salary ranges for positions in these fields?

   - What additional information did you learn during this research?

2. Compose a document by keying paragraphs that address the questions above. Add a meaningful title. Include your name and the date. Proofread, edit, and revise the paragraphs to correct all grammar and spelling errors. Print the document. Proofread it again and make any final changes before submitting it to your instructor.

Numbered and bulleted lists are commonly used to emphasize information in reports, newspapers, magazine articles, and overhead presentations. Review the proper formats for numbered and bulleted lists as described below.

Enumerations and Bulleted Lists

- Parentheses are used to set off numbered lists within a sentence.

- Bullets are typically used when no particular sequence is required; numbers are used for lists that require a sequence of steps or points.

- Bullets can be converted to numbers and numbers converted to bullets by selecting the list and then clicking on the *Bullets* or *Numbering* command for the style desired.

EXAMPLES OF ENUMERATION AND BULLET STYLES

We would like to purchase the following items from your store: (1) five notebooks, (2) ten pens, and (3) two computers.

We had several students enter the contest this year. The following students will be eligible to compete in the Business Excellence Competition for Raymond High School:

- Mary Adams, Freshman
- Sandra Brown, Sophomore
- Randy Sisk, Junior
- Larry Lee, Senior

Before you start to transcribe your documents from the CD, you should be sure to complete the following steps:

1. Read the Learning Objectives for the chapter.
2. Read and study the information in the English Skills Review section.
3. Read and study the information in the Proofreading Tip section.
4. Read and complete the exercises in the English Skills Application section.
5. Read and complete the Composition and Research section.
6. Read and study the Transcription Preview section.

1. Transcribe the Word Mastery terms from the Transcription CD.

2. Transcribe the five documents from the Transcription CD as described below. Key the documents in block letter style with open punctuation and use the current date.

   • Open Document 1 and use the letterhead for At Your Table Catering.

   • Open Document 2 and use the letterhead for Chef Pierre.

   • Open Document 3 and use the letterhead for Kyoto Fantasy Express.

   • Open Document 4 and use the letterhead for The Baltimore City Club.

   • Open Document 5 and use the letterhead for At Your Table Catering.

3. When you have transcribed a document using the file from the Transcription CD, remember to use the **Save As** feature and a distinctive name as the file name for each document.

4. Spell-check, proofread, and submit all five documents to your instructor for approval.

CHAPTER CHECKPOINTS

Place a check mark beside the objectives you can meet after completing this chapter.

_____ I can define, spell, and use the Word Mastery terms in this chapter.

_____ I can use the commonly misused terms from the Word Usage section in this chapter.

_____ I can spell correctly the words in the Spelling section in this chapter.

_____ I can apply the rules for parentheses and capitalization presented in the Language Skills section in this chapter.

_____ I can transcribe documents containing numbered or bulleted lists and proofread carefully.

Evaluation Form

Access the Evaluation Form from your Transcription CD. Complete it and submit it with your work. You may choose to either print the form and complete it or complete the form electronically.

© Darren Baker/Shutterstock.com

Chapter 10

MARKETING, RETAIL, AND WHOLESALE MANAGEMENT

The objective of any firm is to market or sell its products or services. If you enjoy selling and like setting and meeting goals, you should consider a career in the marketing, retail, or wholesale management fields. Many careers in marketing and sales involve a great deal of travel and pressure. A college degree is required for some middle- and upper-management positions.

Word Mastery Preview

Directions: Review the list of Word Mastery terms that will be used in the documents you will be transcribing. Learn the definition for each word and how to spell it correctly.

purchase order	*Definition:*	a request or set of instructions according to which goods or services are sold, made, or furnished
	Example:	When the customer submits a purchase order, we can fill the order.
invoice	*Definition:*	a detailed list of goods sold or services provided including the charges and terms of the sale
	Example:	After the bookkeeper received the invoice, she paid the bill.
receipts	*Definition:*	written acknowledgments of things received
	Example:	When Zackery counted his receipts for his work, he was amazed at the amount of money he had.
customer service	*Definition:*	duties performed professionally with the customer's needs in mind
	Example:	If you don't provide good customer service, your company will lose business.
credit application	*Definition:*	a form that must be completed in order to obtain credit with a company
	Example:	Her credit application was denied because of her poor credit history.
merchandise	*Definition:*	goods or commodities offered for sale
	Example:	Most of the merchandise was stolen.
competitor	*Definition:*	a rival
	Example:	In high school, both sisters were competitors in the beauty contests.
promotion	*Definition:*	the act of advertising or marketing a product or service
	Example:	We did not get the type of promotion we felt our book deserved.

coupon   *Definition:* a detachable portion of a certificate or ticket which entitles the holder to a gift or discount
       Example: Many people receive coupons in the mail.

advertisement   *Definition:* an announcement promoting a product or service
       Example: The advertisement was not in today's newspaper.

quarter   *Definition:* one-fourth of a year
       Example: The sales staff must meet their goals for the quarter.

redeem   *Definition:* to exchange for money or goods
       Example: She redeemed her coupons at the grocery store.

profit margin   *Definition:* the ratio of gain to the amount of capital invested
       Example: Unfortunately, his profit margin was less than he had expected.

overhead   *Definition:* the general cost of running a business
       Example: Your overhead can be reduced if you find creative ways to save money.

B Word Usage

Directions: Learn to spell and define these confusing words, which may occur within the documents you will be transcribing.

ade   (noun) a sweet beverage
aid   (verb or noun) to help or to facilitate; a form of help
aide   (noun) a person who assists

adverse   (adjective) hostile; unfavorable
averse   (adjective) disinclined

aisle   (noun) a passage between rows
isle   (noun) island

desert   (noun or verb) arid, barren land; to abandon
dessert   (noun) the last course of a meal

fair   (noun or adjective) a trade exhibit; just; light in color; unclouded
fare   (noun) the cost to a passenger for transportation; food

raise	(verb or noun) to lift something; increase in pay
raze	(verb) to destroy

receipt	(noun) a written acknowledgment of things received
recipe	(noun) a formula using ingredients

C Spelling

Directions: Learn to spell these common words.

accidentally	disappear	immediately
acknowledgment	excellent	knowledge
benefited	exhausted	mathematics
committed	experience	noticeable
controversy	experiment	supersede

D Language Skills

Directions: Enhance your language skills by reviewing basic grammar, punctuation, capitalization, number/figure style, abbreviation style, and word division rules. Study the rules and examples below.

Rule: Use a comma to set off a nonrestrictive subordinate clause. A nonrestrictive subordinate clause cannot stand alone and is dependent upon the main clause; however, it is not essential to the meaning of the sentence. If the subordinate clause is restrictive and necessary to make the meaning of the sentence clear and complete, do not set it off in commas.

Examples:
- Our new neighbor, who seems very nice, lived in North Dakota before moving to Idaho.
- All students who have an A average at this point in the semester will not have to take the final exam.

Rule: Spell out common fractions appearing alone in ordinary writing. Write mixed numbers as figures.

Examples:
- Over one-fourth of the class was absent yesterday.
- Use 1 1/2 cups of sugar when making the recipe.

Proofreading
Tip

- If you give a reference location in a document, make sure the reference is in the location to which you refer the reader. Can you find the error in the sentence below?

Please look at the rules regarding the use of commas with nonrestrictive subordinate clauses on the next page in this text-workbook.

The rule is not located on the next page, is it? It is located on this page. If you give a page reference or page number in the text you key, check to see that it is the correct location for that reference.

ENGLISH SKILLS EXERCISES

A   Word Mastery

Directions: Apply what you learned in the English Skills Review. Choose the correct word in the following sentences from those found in the Word Mastery Preview.

1. Mail the _purchase order_ today to ensure our supplier ships the equipment soon.

2. One _customer service_ telephone tip is to never leave the customer holding the line for more than 30 seconds at a time.

3. The two students were _____ for the most outstanding student award.

4. You can see a(n) _advertisement_ for your favorite products on television.

5. The first _quarter_ is usually the busiest for accountants.

6. Before you can receive a credit card, you must complete a(n) _credit application_ that requests various information.

7. Because the company's _overhead_ was so expensive, the company had to find ways to cut down on some of its operational costs.

8. Once Janis ordered the crib for her granddaughter, Austin, she received a(n) _invoice_ that lists the amount she owed.

9. Howard and Jane kept all the _receipts_ for the gifts they purchased for Christmas in case they needed to return any of them.

10. The summer _merchandise_ was reduced half price in hopes the boutique could sell it quickly and make room for the fall line.

B   Word Usage

Directions: Choose the correct word in each of the following sentences.

1. What is the (fair, _fare_) to transport this package to the next state?

2. When we (_raise_, raze) the building, we will need to be sure everyone is a safe distance away from the location.

3. My son has an (ade, aid, _aide_) to assist him with his important cases.

4. Of course, you need to make sure there is enough room for shopping carts between each (_aisle_, isle) in the store.

5. If you don't eat all the food on your plate, you cannot have (desert, _dessert_).

6. When you submit your (_receipt_, recipe), you will be reimbursed for the purchases.

7. She is (adverse, _averse_) to our taking on additional marketing strategies at this time.

8. We want to be sure we are implementing (fair, fare) trading agreements.

9. Let's try to give (ade, aid, aide) to the new recruits since they have not had as much training as we have had.

10. While we want to (raise, raze) profits, we have to be careful about increasing the price of our product.

C Spelling

Directions: Choose the correct spelling in each of the following sentences.

1. We (immediately, immediatelly) saw our products sell, and they seemed to (disapear, disappear) off the shelves in the store.

2. If we are all (commited, committed) to the company and its goals, we will (experiance, experience) unity.

3. The marketing campaign was (excellant, excellent); however, all the sales force were (exausted, exhausted).

4. There had been so much (controversy, controversey) regarding the (experement, experiment) that the manager decided not to proceed at the present time.

5. I (accidentaly, accidentally) lost last quarter's report that I was to present to my supervisors.

6. Some type of (acknowledgment, acknowlegement) would have been appreciated by our sponsors for the event.

7. (Knowledge, Knowlege) of marketing and management is a requirement for this supervisory position.

8. J. D. found that basic (mathmatics, mathematics) (benefited, benefitted) him when he was completing the year-end inventory reports.

9. His lack of leadership was (noticeble, noticeable) by all the employees.

10. The directives that we just received will (supercede, supersede) the directives we were given two weeks ago.

D Language Skills

Directions: Use proofreaders' marks to make corrections in the following sentences. Write "Correct" by the sentence if no corrections are needed.

1. Jane put one and a third cups of the liquid into the container.

2. We hope that 2/3 of the class will vote for our friend and not for Hayley.

3. If we check the recipe, we will find that it requires 2 1/2 cups of flour.

4. Jessica Cruise who I think is a wonderful actress had the feature role in the movie.

5. The man, who has the fastest car, will win the race.

6. We will have to reduce the merchandise by 1/3 to try and move it off the floor.

7. All merchandise, that is purchased during the sale, cannot be returned.

8. The sweater, which was so attractive, did not fit Marie properly.

9. The woman who wore the red vest is the manager.

10. Rita Hanks who is a friendly person will be our new manager.

E Composition

1. Compose and key a paragraph applying the word mastery, word usage, spelling, and language skills you have studied.

2. Compose and key a second paragraph that contains your favorite recipe, making sure to use fractions in the ingredients.

3. Compose and key a third paragraph that describes the types of merchandise found in your favorite department store. Include at least one nonrestrictive clause and one restrictive clause in your paragraph and punctuate those clauses correctly. Submit all three paragraphs to your instructor.

F Research

1. Conduct research using the Internet, newspaper, and library or talk with individuals who are actually employed in the marketing, retail, and wholesale management fields to obtain information about the topics listed below. When searching online, go to the U.S. Bureau of Labor Statistics website at **www.bls.gov** and click on the **Publications** tab. Then click on the *Occupational Outlook Handbook* and **Index** links. Click on the first letter of the name of the field. (Example: Click on the letter *M* and scroll down the screen to find information on *marketing*.) You can also do an online search of the name of the field/industry followed by the words *career* or *training*. (Example: *marketing career* or *marketing training*)

   • What are the employment opportunities for office workers in the marketing, retail, and wholesale management fields?

   • What are the advantages and/or disadvantages of employment in these fields?

   • What skills or characteristics are necessary for someone who wants to work in these fields?

   • What are the job titles or positions in these fields?

   • What are the salary ranges for positions in these fields?

   • What additional information did you learn during this research?

2. Compose a document by keying paragraphs that address the questions above. Add a meaningful title. Include your name and the date. Proofread, edit, and revise the paragraphs to correct all grammar and spelling errors. Print the document. Proofread it again and make any final changes before submitting it to your instructor.

Whole Numbers, Fractions, and Mixed Numbers

- Whole numbers (0, 1, 2, 3, etc.) are integers or counting numbers and do not include any fractions.

- Fractions (one-fourth, one-third, one-half, etc.) are less than a whole number.

- Mixed numbers (1 1/4, 2 1/3, 3 1/2, etc.) include whole numbers with fractions. Note that fractions are written in figure format when they are part of a mixed number; the fractions include a numerator (number on top) and denominator (number on bottom).

- When you key 1/2, Microsoft Word will automatically print it as ½. When you key 1/4, it will automatically print as ¼. All other fractions will remain as keyed; for example, 1/3 will remain 1/3. Therefore, if you are using various mixed numbers in one sentence, it is best that they are uniform in appearance. If you have 1 1/3 in the same sentence as 2 ½, delete the ½ in 2 ½ and rekey it as 2 1/2. You can also hit the backspace key immediately after keying ½ or ¼, and the fraction will be changed to 1/2 or 1/4.

TRANSCRIPTION EXERCISES

1. Transcribe the Word Mastery terms from the Transcription CD.

2. Transcribe the five documents from the Transcription CD following the instructions below and using the current date.

    - Open Document 1 and use the letterhead for Mom and Pop's Texan Apparel. Key this document in memorandum format.

    - Open Document 2 and use the letterhead for Town and Country Casuals. Key this document in block letter style with open punctuation.

    - Open Document 3 and use the letterhead for Omaha Wholesale Grocery. Key this document in block letter style with open punctuation.

    - Open Document 4 and use the letterhead for Barton's Retail. Key this document in memorandum format.

    - Open Document 5 and use the letterhead for Town and Country Casuals. Key this document in block letter style with open punctuation.

3. When you have transcribed a document using the file from the Transcription CD, remember to use the **Save As** feature and a distinctive name as the file name for each document.

4. Spell-check, proofread, and submit all five documents to your instructor for approval.

CHAPTER CHECKPOINTS

Place a check mark beside the objectives
you can meet after completing this chapter.

_____ I can define, spell, and use the Word Mastery terms in this chapter.

_____ I can use the commonly misused terms from the Word Usage section in this chapter.

_____ I can spell correctly the words in the Spelling section in this chapter.

_____ I can apply the rules for commas presented in the Language Skills section in this chapter.

_____ I can apply the rules for number/figure style presented in the Language Skills section in this chapter.

_____ I can transcribe documents containing whole numbers, fractions, and mixed numbers and proofread carefully.

*Evaluation Form

Access the Evaluation Form from your Transcription CD. Complete it and submit it with your work. You may choose to either print the form and complete it or complete the form electronically.

© michaeljung/Shutterstock.com

Chapter 11

TRAVEL, TOURISM, AND HOTEL SERVICES

Employment opportunities in the travel, tourism, and hotel services industries may be found in travel agencies, motels, hotels, resorts, and airports. Some positions have minimal entry requirements; other positions require post-secondary training or college degrees. Although these industries can be exciting and seem glamorous, long work hours and odd shifts are usually required. High stress levels are common in many positions in these industries.

ENGLISH SKILLS REVIEW

 A **Word Mastery Preview**

Directions: Review the list of Word Mastery terms that will be used in the documents you will be transcribing. Learn the definition for each word and how to spell it correctly.

arrangements	*Definition:*	preparations
	Example:	Last-minute arrangements had to be made before the wedding.
conference	*Definition:*	a meeting for consultation or discussion
	Example:	After the conference, all the participants knew what the company expected them to achieve in the next year.
accommodations	*Definition:*	lodging arrangements
	Example:	Because no accommodations had been arranged, they did not have a room for the night.
confirmed	*Definition:*	verified
	Example:	Lauren confirmed her appointment with her physician.
ninety	*Definition:*	ten times nine
	Example:	She had lived ninety years before she became ill.
occupancy	*Definition:*	amount of space allowed
	Example:	The maximum occupancy for the room is 125 people.
customized	*Definition:*	made to individual orders
	Example:	After his measurements were taken, the tailor customized the suit for him.
inquiry	*Definition:*	a question
	Example:	Please send your inquiry about this position to the supervisor.

| authentic | *Definition:* | genuine or real |
| | *Example:* | Her jewelry was not authentic. |

| itinerary | *Definition:* | a detailed plan for a trip or visit |
| | *Example:* | If you would like a copy of Ivan's itinerary so you can contact him while he is gone, please let me know. |

| attractions | *Definition:* | people or things that draw attention |
| | *Example:* | When you are on your vacation, be sure to see as many attractions as you can. |

| questionnaire | *Definition:* | a list of questions producing replies that can be analyzed |
| | *Example:* | When you complete the enclosed questionnaire, send it to us immediately. |

| bed and breakfast inn | *Definition:* | accommodations other than a hotel/motel that provide lodging and the morning meal for guests |
| | *Example:* | Some people find bed and breakfast inns more intimate than the larger hotel and motel chains. |

| cuisine | *Definition:* | food |
| | *Example:* | The South is known for having wonderful cuisine. |

| pedicure | *Definition:* | professional treatment or care of the feet |
| | *Example:* | Wanda enjoyed the pedicure she received from the salon. |

| manicure | *Definition:* | professional treatment or care of the hands |
| | *Example:* | After seeing how attractive her hands looked, Savita decided to have a manicure once a week. |

| reservation | *Definition:* | secured arrangements |
| | *Example:* | Be sure you make your reservation for the business trip. |

| confirmation | *Definition:* | valid or proven |
| | *Example:* | She did not ask for her confirmation number. |

B Word Usage

Directions: Learn to spell and define these confusing words, which may occur within the documents you will be transcribing.

beach	(noun) a place near the ocean
beech	(adjective) a type of tree

boar	(noun) a wild pig
boor	(noun) a rude person
bore	(noun or verb) something that is devoid of interest; to tire or weary or to drill

boarder	(noun) a lodger whose meals are included
border	(noun) a perimeter

galley	(noun) a ship's kitchen
gally	(verb) to frighten or terrify

grease	(noun) lubricant
Greece	(noun) a Mediterranean country

hostel	(noun) inexpensive lodging for travelers
hostile	(adjective) unfriendly

loch	(noun) a lake
lock	(noun) a security device

C Spelling

Directions: Learn to spell these common words.

acquaintance	Caribbean	foreign
allegiance	citizen	memento
almost	comfortable	occurrence
beginning	embarrass	tomatoes
breathe	fascinating	traveling

D Language Skills

Directions: Enhance your language skills by reviewing basic grammar, punctuation, capitalization, number/figure style, abbreviation style, and word division rules. Study the rules and examples below.

Rule:	Use parentheses to enclose figures verifying a number that is spelled out.
Examples:	• I owe him twenty-five dollars ($25).
	• Jim's utility bill for one hundred fifty dollars ($150) was much lower than last month's bill.

Rule:	Capitalize the proper names of states, motels and hotels, businesses, and cultural or entertainment facilities. Common names are not capitalized.
Examples:	• I will visit Idaho and stay at the Idaho Inn while I attend the Idaho State Fair.
	• After visiting the city park in his home state, Shane spent the night at the hotel.

ENGLISH SKILLS EXERCISES

A Word Mastery

Directions: Apply what you learned in the English Skills Review. Choose the correct word in the following sentences from those found in the Word Mastery Preview.

1. He hoped he could attend the _____ that was to be held in North Dakota.

2. Because of fire codes, the _____ of the elevator was limited to ten people.

3. Your _____ regarding this matter will be directed to our manager.

4. Yoko kept a copy of her employer's _____ available while her employer was traveling.

Word Mastery (continued)

5. A(n) _____ can provide valuable feedback to researchers.

6. Be sure you made your _____ for your hotel room.

7. Many people prefer to stay at a(n) _____ instead of some of the large hotel and motel chains.

8. Many restaurants are known for their fine _____.

9. Because Rico did not like the _____ the hotel desk clerk made for him, he requested another room.

10. Marbella wanted to add a(n) _____ to her day at the spa when she finished having her manicure.

B Word Usage

Directions: Choose the correct word in each of the following sentences.

1. When we traveled to (grease, Greece) last year, we had the best vacation of our lives.

2. If you go to Europe, the most affordable place to get a room is in a local (hostel, hostile).

3. Put a (loch, lock) on your safety deposit box.

4. The lecture was such a (boar, boor, bore) that most of the class fell asleep.

5. We love the (beach, beech) so much that we go four times a year.

6. My great-grandmother used to take in a (boarder, border) to help make ends meet financially.

7. She was so (hostel, hostile) that no one wanted to be around her.

8. The (boarder, border) between our property and the new hotel's property is lined with trees.

9. Her new kitchen is so narrow and small that it reminds me of a (galley, gally).

10. The cat decided to climb up the (beach, beech) tree in our backyard.

C Spelling

Directions: Choose the correct spelling in each of the following sentences.

1. When we visited the (Caribbean, Carribean) last summer, we saw lots of shells on the beach.

2. If you do a great deal of (traveling, travelling), you will want to get a (memento, momento) from every place you visit.

3. As Peggy was trying to communicate with the (citizen, citizin) from a (foreign, foriegn) country, she realized he understood English very well.

4. (Allmost, Almost) every time we stay at the Plaza International Hotel, we find our accommodations to be excellent.

5. She was so allergic from eating the (tomatoes, tomatos) that she could hardly (breath, breathe).

6. (Beginning, Begining) the first of next month, we will be checking the cleanliness of the rooms more carefully.

7. Every (occurrance, occurrence) was so infrequent that she cherished the times she could visit family.

8. Does it (embarass, embarrass) you when you encounter an old (acquaintance, acquaintence) and can't remember his or her name?

9. Visiting different places can be so (facinating, fascinating) because you meet new people, taste different cuisines, and see new sights.

10. Although I have lived in several countries, my (allegiance, allegence) will always be with America because I was born there many years ago and hope to return soon.

D Language Skills

Directions: Use proofreaders' marks to make corrections in the following sentences. Write "Correct" by the sentence if no corrections are needed.

1. Harrison hoped his grandmother would send him twenty dollars ($20) for his birthday.

2. I plan to spend thirty dollars $30 on his wedding gift.

3. Don't you want to go to the Baseball Stadium this afternoon?

4. After seeing Yankee Stadium, I knew I wanted to be a baseball player.

5. Let's visit the City Zoo next month.

6. If you want to reserve the room, the rate will be seventy dollars ($70) per night.

7. We will need to visit the Washington memorial when we are in Washington.

8. Does her son work at the state park?

9. Of course, we will visit the Florida state park when we go on vacation.

10. We don't usually enjoy eating at seafood restaurants, but we did enjoy eating at Captain Eddie's Seafood Palace.

E Composition

1. Compose and key a paragraph applying the word mastery, word usage, spelling, and language skills you have studied.

2. Compose and key a second paragraph in which you plan a business conference at your school for the 15th and 16th of next month. Include an itinerary.

3. Compose and key a third paragraph in which you confirm a hotel reservation. Submit all three paragraphs to your instructor.

F Research

1. Conduct research using the Internet, newspaper, and library or talk with individuals who are actually employed in the travel, tourism, and hotel services fields to obtain information about the topics listed below. When searching online, go to the U.S. Bureau of Labor Statistics website at **www.bls.gov** and click on the **Publications** tab. Then click on the ***Occupational Outlook Handbook*** and **Index** links. Click on the first letter of the name of the field. (Example: Click on the letter *T* and scroll down the screen to find information on *travel*.) You can also do an online search of the name of the field/industry followed by the words *career* or *training*. (Example: *travel career* or *travel training*)

    - What are the employment opportunities for office workers in the travel, tourism, and hotel services fields?

    - What are the advantages and/or disadvantages of employment in these fields?

    - What skills or characteristics are necessary for someone who wants to work in these fields?

    - What are the job titles or positions in these fields?

    - What are the salary ranges for positions in these fields?

    - What additional information did you learn during this research?

2. Compose a document by keying paragraphs that address the questions above. Add a meaningful title. Include your name and the date. Proofread, edit, and revise the paragraphs to correct all grammar and spelling errors. Print the document. Proofread it again and make any final changes before submitting it to your instructor.

TRANSCRIPTION PREVIEW

Use attention lines to get the attention of a certain department (for example: Personnel Department) or a certain position (for example: Personnel Director) within a company. Review the proper format for attention lines as described below and on the next page.

Attention Lines

- Key the attention line as the first line of the letter address.

- Use *Dear* followed by the name of the position title as the salutation if the position title is used in the attention line.

- Use *Ladies* and *Gentlemen* as the salutation if the department or division is used in the attention line.

Attention Personnel Director   ⟵ Attention line
XYZ Company
34 South Broad Street   ⟵ Letter address
Greenville, SC 29605

Dear Personnel Director   ⟵ Salutation

or

Attention Personnel Department ⟵ Attention line
XYZ Company
34 Broad Street   ⟵ Letter address
Greenville, SC 29605

Ladies and Gentlemen   ⟵ Salutation

TRANSCRIPTION EXERCISES

1. Transcribe the Word Mastery terms from the Transcription CD.

2. Transcribe the five documents from the Transcription CD as described below. Key the documents in block letter style with open punctuation and use the current date.

   - Open Document 1 and use the letterhead for Tampa Tour Company.

   - Open Document 2 and use the letterhead for Wyoming Travel Group.

   - Open Document 3 and use the letterhead for The Hide-Away.

   - Open Document 4 and use the letterhead for Peach State Travel Agency.

   - Open Document 5 and use the letterhead for Wyoming Travel Group.

3. When you have transcribed a document using the file from the Transcription CD, remember to use the **Save As** feature and a distinctive name as the file name for each document.

4. Spell-check, proofread, and submit all five documents to your instructor for approval.

CHAPTER CHECKPOINTS

Place a check mark beside the objectives
you can meet after completing this chapter.

_____ I can define, spell, and use the Word Mastery terms in this chapter.

_____ I can use the commonly misused terms from the Word Usage section in this chapter.

_____ I can spell correctly the words in the Spelling section in this chapter.

_____ I can apply the rules for parentheses presented in the Language Skills section in this chapter.

_____ I can apply the rules for capitalization presented in the Language Skills section in this chapter.

_____ I can transcribe documents containing attention lines and proofread carefully.

Evaluation Form

Access the Evaluation Form from your Transcription CD. Complete it and submit it with your work. You may choose to either print the form and complete it or complete the form electronically.

© Creatas/Jupiter Images

Chapter 12

AIRLINE, AUTOMOTIVE, AND TRUCKING INDUSTRIES

Within the airline, automotive, and trucking industries, there are many types of positions from which you may choose. Sales staff, customer service representatives, mechanics, and operators are among some of the diverse positions that may interest you. Although some positions require only a high school diploma, other positions require post-secondary or college training. Other positions require specialized training and licensing. Traffic and transportation industries must meet state and federal regulations.

ENGLISH SKILLS REVIEW

 A **Word Mastery Preview**

Directions: Review the list of Word Mastery terms that will be used in the documents you will be transcribing. Learn the definition for each word and how to spell it correctly.

boarding	*Definition:*	the act of entering a plane, ship, or train
	Example:	As she was boarding the plane, she fell and broke her leg.
destination	*Definition:*	the place to which a person or thing travels or is sent
	Example:	When she planned her trip, her final destination was Alaska.
charter	*Definition:*	reserve for a special purpose
	Example:	The team wanted to fly by charter service rather than commercial service.
interstate	*Definition:*	involving movement between states
	Example:	The United States Government allows interstate commerce.
license	*Definition:*	a formal permission from a constituted authority to do a special thing
	Example:	Rebecca was excited when she received her driver's license.
analysis	*Definition:*	the process of studying the nature of something
	Example:	After much analysis, the company decided to cut labor costs.
replenish	*Definition:*	to make full or complete again
	Example:	After most of the office supplies were used, the office professional wanted to replenish the supply cabinet.
inventory	*Definition:*	merchandise, materials, or stock on hand
	Example:	Much of the company's inventory was damaged in the fire.
vehicles	*Definition:*	equipment used to move or carry something
	Example:	Several vehicles were stolen from the parking lot.

model	*Definition:*	the type of vehicle such as two-door or four-door
	Example:	Because they had several children, the couple decided on the four-door model rather than the two-door model.

make	*Definition:*	the manufacturer of the vehicle such as Ford or Dodge
	Example:	He indicated that the make of his car is a BMW.

inspection	*Definition:*	examination
	Example:	We no longer perform inspections on our automobiles.

log	*Definition:*	various detailed records of the operation of a vehicle
	Example:	Because he had lost his log, Jim could not complete his travel expense report.

dispatched	*Definition:*	to send off with efficiency
	Example:	He dispatched the taxi immediately.

B Word Usage

Directions: Learn to spell and define these confusing words, which may occur within the documents you will be transcribing.

access	(noun or verb) admittance; to get into
excess	(noun) abundance

choose	(verb) to select
chose	(verb) past tense of the verb *choose*

coarse	(adjective) rough
course	(noun) a subject of study

cue	(noun) a hint or a signal
queue	(noun) a waiting line of people or objects

farther	(adjective or adverb) a measurable distance
further	(adjective or adverb) more; in addition

hour	(noun) sixty minutes
our	(pronoun) belonging to us
are	(verb) a form of the verb to be

wares	(noun) goods
wears	(verb) puts on

 **Spelling**

Directions: Learn to spell these common words.

absence	diesel	preferred
accounting	fulfill	receive
achievement	inconvenient	truly
conscientious	judgment	undoubtedly
description	parallel	weight

 Language Skills

Directions: Enhance your language skills by reviewing basic grammar, punctuation, capitalization, number/figure style, abbreviation style, and word division rules. Study the rules and examples below.

Proofreading Tip

- As you proofread any document you have keyed, be sure parallel ideas are expressed in parallel form. For example, adjectives should be paralleled by adjectives, nouns by nouns, infinitives by infinitives, etc. What is wrong in the following example?

Rachel likes to file papers, answering the phone, and keying documents.

To file is an infinitive (to + a verb); *answering* and *keying* are gerunds (form of a verb that ends in "ing"). Both of the following sentences use parallel structure, and either is acceptable.

Rachel likes to file papers, to answer the phone, and to key documents.

Rachel likes filing papers, answering the phone, and keying documents.

Rule: Use a hyphen to show passage of time, except when used with the words *from* or *between*.

Examples:
- Boarding time is scheduled for 1:30-2:00 p.m.
- People holding tickets may board the ferry between 1:30 and 2:00 p.m.
- Juan lived in Chicago from 1998 to 1999.

Rule: Capitalize proper names of cities, states, rivers, mountains, etc. Common nouns are not capitalized.

Examples:
- Mount Waialeale is on Kauai in the Hawaiian Islands.
- We hope to raft many rivers and to climb several mountains in the western states this summer.

Rule: Capitalize compass directions when they are used to name a particular part of the country. Do not capitalize these words when they merely indicate a general location or direction.

Examples:
- To view the best colors in the East, travel north through the state on I-91.

- People in the Southwest don't seem to have the allergies that people in the Southeast do.

- Emma lives on the west side of our town.

ENGLISH SKILLS EXERCISES

 ### A Word Mastery

Directions: Apply what you learned in the English Skills Review. Choose the correct word in the following sentences from those found in the Word Mastery Preview.

1. The couple left for their honeymoon; however, no one knew their actual
   _____.

2. You will need to _____ the paper in your printer.

3. As we unpacked the _____, we noticed that some of the equipment had been lost.

4. Upon further _____ Jolene discovered that the table had been damaged.

5. He _____ the ambulance as soon as he received the 911 call.

6. Many _____ were on the car lot for sale.

7. When people purchase automobiles, they want to select the _____ that suits their family's needs.

8. If your parent's drove a certain _____ of automobile, you probably tend to purchase from the same manufacturer.

9. Delivery drivers have to keep a(n) _____ of the mileage they complete.

10. _____ travel between states can be dangerous.

B Word Usage

Directions: Choose the correct word in each of the following sentences.

1. You will need to drive a little (farther, further) to reach our destination.

2. Because we received a (cue, queue), we were able to apprehend the victim.

3. Of course, we will (choose, chose) the right person for the supervisory position.

4. Since there had been a large harvest that year, there was an (access, excess) of produce to deliver to market.

Word Usage (continued)

5. All the trucks were told to assemble in a (cue, queue) at the weight station.

6. After he loaded all the (wares, wears) onto his tractor trailer, he drove to Mississippi.

7. We were not aware that (hour, our, are) shipment was delayed for more than an (hour, our, are).

8. Do you want (farther, further) information about becoming a flight attendant?

9. My child was not allowed (access, excess) to his test scores.

10. I (choose, chose) not to be a participant in the competition held last week.

C Spelling

Directions: Choose the correct spelling in each of the following sentences.

1. The truck driver filled up his tank with (deisel, diesel) fuel right before he had to enter the (waight, weight) station.

2. The owner (perferred, preferred) that cars not be parked (parralel, parallel) to the building.

3. Our (accounting, accountting) manager (undoubtedly, undoutally) will double check all the figures in our report.

4. Because he is so (consentous, conscientious), his (acheivement, achievement) is not a surprise to me.

5. Students cannot (receive, recieve) the perfect attendance award if they have had an (absence, absense) during the year.

6. What (description, discription) for the suspect did he give the police officer?

7. Allen used poor (judgement, judgment) when he decided to take the shorter route than the one he was given.

8. After all the students had submitted their work, the instructor was (truely, truly) amazed at what they had learned.

9. Don't you want to (fulfil, fulfill) your lifelong goal by graduating from college?

10. Although it was (inconvenent, inconvenient) for J.C., he decided to drive his friend to the airport before his flight.

D Language Skills

Directions: Use proofreaders' marks to make corrections in the following sentences. Write "Correct" by the sentence if no corrections are needed.

1. We will hold our meeting from 1:30–3:30 p.m.

2. We can see you between 9:00 and 10:30 a.m. today.

3. Don't you think the people in the south are friendly?

4. Her office faces West; his office faces East.

5. She stopped by the Mississippi river to see the steamboats.

6. The flight was 3:00 to 4:30 p.m.

7. We drove past the state line.

8. Marcela drove North to see her family.

9. Rico lived in the south all his life.

10. Don't you think we should visit the State Capital on our next road trip?

E Composition

1. Compose and key a paragraph applying the word mastery, word usage, spelling, and language skills you have studied.

2. Compose and key a second paragraph describing a trip to your favorite destination and include a time schedule utilizing hyphens.

3. Compose and key a third paragraph about the interstate nearest you and use compass directions in the paragraph. Submit all three paragraphs to your instructor.

F Research

1. Conduct research using the Internet, newspaper, and library or talk with individuals who are actually employed in the airline, automotive, and trucking fields to obtain information about the topics listed below. When searching online, go to the U.S. Bureau of Labor Statistics website at **www.bls.gov** and click on the **Publications** tab. Then click on the *Occupational Outlook Handbook* and **Index** links. Click on the first letter of the name of the field. (Example: Click on the letter *A* and scroll down the screen to find information on *airlines.*) You can also do an online search of the name of the field/industry followed by the words *career* or *training*. (Example: *airline career* or *airline training*)

    • What are the employment opportunities for office workers in the airline, automotive, or trucking industries?

    • What are the advantages and/or disadvantages of employment in these fields?

    • What skills or characteristics are necessary for someone who wants to work in these fields?

    • What are the job titles or positions in these fields?

    • What are the salary ranges for positions in these fields?

    • What additional information did you learn during this research?

2. Compose and key paragraphs that address the questions above. Add a meaningful title. Include your name and the date. Proofread, edit, and revise the paragraphs to correct all grammar and spelling errors. Print the document. Proofread it again and make any final changes before submitting it to your instructor.

TRANSCRIPTION PREVIEW

Tables make it easy to present data and graphics in a document. Tables contain columns (vertical lists of information from left to right), rows (horizontal lists of information from top to bottom), and cells (an intersection of a column and a row). Review the proper format for tables described below.

Tables

- If the table is keyed within a document, begin the table by tapping ENTER once after the previous line of text. If the table is not part of a document, center it horizontally and vertically.
- Key main headings in 14-point, bold font, all caps.
- Key secondary headings in 12-point, bold font, and capitalize the first letter of each main word.
- Key column headings in 11-point, bold font, and capitalize the first letter of each main word.
- Key the table text in 11-point font at the left of each cell unless it is a monetary amount, which should be aligned at the decimal.
- Change the row height to .3″.
- Remove all the borders of the table.

Main heading → **BRIGHTON COLLEGE AOT 101 – 108 CLASSES**

Secondary heading → **Fall 20--**

Subject	Time of Class	Location	Instructor's Name
AOT 101	8:00 – 8:50 a.m., MWF	Room 200	Ballard
AOT 102	8:00 – 8:50 a.m., MWF	Room 201	Custer
AOT 103	8:00 – 8:50 a.m., MWF	Room 202	Dillard
AOT 104	8:00 – 8:50 a.m., MWF	Room 203	Edwards
AOT 105	9:00 – 9:50 a.m., MWF	Room 200	Ballard
AOT 106	9:00 – 9:50 a.m., MWF	Room 201	Custer
AOT 107	9:00 – 9:50 a.m., MWF	Room 202	Dillard
AOT 108	9:00 – 9:50 a.m., MWF	Room 203	Edwards

Column headings · Table text

1. Transcribe the Word Mastery terms from the Transcription CD.

2. Transcribe the five documents from the Transcription CD following the instructions below and using the current date.

   • Open Document 1 and use plain paper. Key this in table format.

   • Open Document 2 and use the letterhead for Washington Airlines. Key this letter in block style with open punctuation.

   • Open Document 3 and use the letterhead for Mendez Rentals. Key this letter in block style with open punctuation.

   • Open Document 4 and use the letterhead for Fitzgerald Trucking Lines. Key this in memorandum format.

   • Open Document 5 and use plain paper. Key this in table format.

3. When you have transcribed a document using the file from the Transcription CD, remember to use the **Save As** feature and a distinctive file name.

4. Spell-check, proofread, and submit all five documents to your instructor.

CHAPTER CHECKPOINTS

Place a check mark beside the objectives
you can meet after completing this chapter.

_____ I can define, spell, and use the Word Mastery terms in this chapter.

_____ I can use the commonly misused terms from the Word Usage section in this chapter.

_____ I can spell correctly the words in the Spelling section in this chapter.

_____ I can apply the rules for hyphenation and capitalization presented in the Language Skills section in this chapter.

_____ I can transcribe documents containing tables and proofread carefully.

Evaluation Form

Access the Evaluation Form from your Transcription CD. Complete it and submit it with your work. You may choose to either print the form and complete it or complete the form electronically.

IMPORTANT NOTE: Check with your instructor regarding the testing procedures for Part 2 (Chapters 7–12).

PART 3
Advanced Machine Transcription–Legal and Medical

Why did you decide to do this type of work?

"When my husband and I moved to Greenville in 1986 with two small children, I decided that I wanted to go back to school and earn a degree. I wanted to have a career and be able to contribute financially to our family. I decided on the Secretarial Science Program (now called Automated Office Technology) at Greenville Technical College."

Who inspired you to consider working in transcription?

"I did not have anyone who actually inspired me. It just happened to be part of the job."

Where did you learn how to transcribe?

"I learned through some of the training received in my courses at Greenville Technical College. Most of my experience has been through working."

How did you educationally prepare for your current position?

"The courses through Greenville Technical College were my base training. Experience through previous job positions has also been very helpful. I am a member of the International Association of Administrative Professionals (IAAP), which was formerly known as Professional Secretaries International (PSI). My IAAP membership provides me with education and training through seminars and programs sponsored by IAAP. I also obtained my Certified Professional Secretary (CPS) rating by attending review courses offered through Furman University and taking a six-part exam. I continue to keep my CPS rating current with the educational opportunities offered through IAAP membership."

> *When you have a person who is good at dictating, you can almost develop a rhythm while keying.*

What do you enjoy the most and the least about transcribing?

"Transcribing is often much easier than trying to read handwritten notes. When you have a person who is good at dictating, you can almost develop a rhythm while keying. On the flip side, there are those people who are not good at dictating. They do not speak clearly and stop and start several times, making it hard to understand what they are actually saying. This can be challenging when transcribing."

What advice would you give a student regarding transcription?

"Transcription is a good skill to have. I have used it for many years in different job positions. There are many offices in which it plays a big role."

© Gina Sanders/Shutterstock.com

Chapter 13

CONTINGENCY FEE AGREEMENT, CERTIFICATE OF NOTARY, AND PROBATE COURT FORM

The legal system affects many aspects of our lives because laws define the rules of society. The legal system can be divided into two areas, private law and public law. Private law (also called civil law) governs the relationships among members of a community. Public law is concerned with matters such as constitutional, administrative, and criminal law. Law firms can be small or large; some large law firms have several offices in various locations. Machine transcription is used within the legal community. Therefore, the next four chapters of this text-workbook will be directed to this specialty.

ENGLISH SKILLS REVIEW

A Word Mastery Preview

Directions: Review the list of word mastery terms that will be used in the documents you will be transcribing. Learn the definition for each word and how to spell it correctly.

contingency fee	*Definition:*	an attorney's fee based on a percentage of the amount of money recovered in a legal action
	Example:	The lawyer agreed to accept a contingency fee rather than a fee based on an hourly rate.
attorney	*Definition:*	generally, someone qualified and given the authority to act in another's behalf; specifically, a lawyer
	Example:	Because he was being sued by the motorist who hit him, Ramon asked his attorney to represent him in the case.
Certificate of Notary	*Definition:*	a document containing the facts sworn to be true before someone legally authorized to certify the document
	Example:	When Elena signed the Certificate of Notary, she swore that she had told the truth.
Notary Public	*Definition:*	someone legally authorized to administer oaths and certify documents
	Example:	Jarmaine presented the document to be signed to the Notary Public.
acknowledged	*Definition:*	to have declared or admitted that something is true
	Example:	Rudie acknowledged that Linda's statement was true.
seal	*Definition:*	a pledge or promise
	Example:	A written or spoken seal secures a document in an abstract manner just as wax or glue secures a document in a physical manner.
instrument	*Definition:*	any formal legal document
	Example:	The Certificate of Notary is an example of an instrument used within our legal system.

testimony	*Definition:*	evidence presented by a witness under oath in a court of law
	Example:	Before her case was settled, Patty was prepared to give testimony.

probate	*Definition:*	the legal process of proving that a will is valid or genuine
	Example:	Charlene's will has been admitted into probate court.

will	*Definition:*	the legal declaration for the distribution of one's property and possessions after death
	Example:	In her will, Alice's mother left her brother everything except the house and the land.

decedent	*Definition:*	a person who has died
	Example:	Mail continued to arrive, addressed to the decedent, in the months following the funeral.

witnesses	*Definition:*	people who observe and acknowledge in writing the execution of an instrument
	Example:	By signing her name to the Certificate of Notary, the Notary Public is a witness to everything Sandy declared.

Word Usage

Directions: Learn to spell and define these confusing words, which may occur within the documents you will be transcribing.

adapt	(verb) to adjust
adept	(adjective) skillful or proficient
adopt	(verb) to choose and take

allowed	(verb) to permit
aloud	(adverb) audibly

canvas	(noun) a rough cloth
canvass	(verb) to solicit votes or opinions

elicit	(verb) to draw forth
illicit	(adjective) unlawful

loose	(verb or adjective) to release; not tight
lose	(verb) to suffer the loss of

respectfully	(adverb) in a manner showing special regard
respectively	(adverb) in the order indicated

waive	(verb) to give up
wave	(noun or verb) a gesture; to swing back and forth

 Spelling

Directions: Learn to spell these common words.

acquisition	facsimile	neighbor
allege	hindrance	optimism
campaign	initiative	persistent
deceive	knowledgeable	prominent
efficient	license	sacrifice

D Language Skills

Special Note Regarding Chapters 13-20: *Because these chapters are considered the advanced phase of your machine transcription training, you will be asked to review some language skills from previous chapters and apply them within these chapters in addition to the new language skills presented in each chapter. Thus, you may want to review the language skills you have studied in previous chapters. A summary of all the language skills rules is in the reference manual in the back of this text-workbook.*

Directions: Enhance your language skills by reviewing basic grammar, punctuation, capitalization, number/figure style, abbreviation style, and word division rules. Study the rules and examples below.

Rule: When keying a legal document, use all capital letters for the names of the parties to a legal agreement.

Examples:
- The plaintiff, SHIRLEY NEELY, is a resident of the State of Colorado. (Sentence in a legal document.)
- CHRIS THOMPSON was the decedent's wife. (Sentence in a legal document.)

Rule: Do not divide a one-syllable word.

Examples: • bound • shipped • wrapped

Proofreading Tips

- Check the ending of lines and the beginning of lines to make sure there are no duplications or omissions. What is wrong in the lines below?

I asked my clients to give me all the information they had regarding the case case because I could not represent them if they were not totally open and and honest with me.

Notice that the word *case* and the word *and* ended lines and also began the next lines. Unfortunately, when we see the end of a line or end of a page, it causes us to lose our concentration and become careless in proofreading.

- Check the ending of a page and the beginning of the next page to make sure there are no duplications or omissions.

Language Skills (*continued*)

Rule: Divide a word between syllables if you can leave at least three characters on the first line and carry three characters to the next line. (A mark of punctuation such as a hyphen, a comma, or a period may count as one of the characters.)

Examples:
- thought-ful

- re-ceive (three characters *r*, *e*, and the hyphen on one line and more than three characters carried to the next line)

- anoth-er (cannot be divided at this point because three characters are not carried to the next line; an-other would be acceptable)

- defender. [can be divided two ways: de-fender. (three characters *d*, *e*, and the hyphen on one line and more than three characters carried to the next line); defend-er. (more than three characters on one line and three characters *e*, *r*, and the period on the next line)]

- a-way (cannot be divided because you cannot place at least three characters on the first line)

ENGLISH SKILLS EXERCISES

A Word Mastery

Directions: Apply what you learned in the English Skills Review. Choose the correct word in the following sentences from those found in the Word Mastery Preview.

1. She went to see her _____ for legal advice.

2. Greg _____ yesterday that the person who had testified did not give all the facts in the case.

3. Because his _____ was necessary in the case, he was required to be present the day of the trial.

4. Be sure that we have our _____ kept in a safe place where they can be located easily in case of death.

5. The _____ had no living relatives.

6. Some legal documents need to have the signature of a(n) _____ to certify the documents.

7. We will have to call several _____ to the stand during the trial to state what they observed during the accident.

8. When someone dies, his or her will must go through _____ to prove it is a valid will.

9. Rather than charging his client an hourly rate, Jonathan Carroll and his client settled on a(n) _____.

10. A Contingency Fee Agreement is a legal document or _____ used in our legal system.

B Word Usage

Directions: Choose the correct word in each of the following sentences.

1. Why don't you (canvas, canvass) the neighborhood to see if anybody is (adapt, adept, adopt) in repairing a flat tire.

2. Will pets be (allowed, aloud) in the hotel where we are staying for vacation this summer?

3. He is probably going to (elicit, illicit) your help in teaching the three-year-old class at his church.

4. Did you (loose, lose) your wallet?

5. Many young people today do not treat their professors (respectfully, respectively).

6. The judge decided to (waive, wave) the $25 fine.

7. Rachel never thought her husband was involved in (elicit, illicit) activities.

8. Although she rehearsed her speech several times in her mind, Emma Logan decided to practice one more time by saying the words (allowed, aloud).

9. When you marry, you will have to (adapt, adept, adopt) to someone else's routine.

10. The artist purchased a new (canvas, canvass) to use for her self portrait.

C Spelling

Directions: Choose the correct spelling in each of the following sentences.

1. The judge was a (promenent, prominent) member of society who happened to be my (neighber, neighbor).

2. Although the young couple agreed they would have to (sacrifice, sacrifise) eating out in order to save money for a new home, they were determined to be (persistant, persistent) and meet their goal.

3. When you run for public office, you better be (knowledgeable, knowlegeable) of all aspects of your (campaign, campain).

4. The (facimile, facsimile) was so realistic that it could (deceive, decieve) you at first glance.

5. Because she was so full of (optimisim, optimism), she was determined that any (hindrance, hindrence) that came her way would not dampen her spirits.

6. They (aledge, allege) that the defendant broke into their home on the night of June 5 around 11 p.m.

7. The young teenager was excited to finally obtain his driver's (license, lisence).

Spelling (continued)

8. Because the new (acquisition, aquisition) was so costly, the senior officers of the company decided they could not give any raises to their employees.

9. If you would take the (initiative, initative) to study at least one hour a day, you would make better grades in this course.

10. Why can't you be more (effecient, efficient) like your older sister?

D Language Skills

Directions: Use proofreaders' marks to make corrections in the following sentences. Write "Correct" by the sentence if no corrections are needed. Some of these sentences include a review of language skills presented in previous chapters. You may want to refer to the reference manual in the back of this text-workbook for a review before completing these examples.

1. Jeremy Johnson furnished the correct information regarding the rental of the premises. (Sentence in a legal document.)

2. The details of her divorce were not given to me.

3. The attorney of course kept his client informed of all aspects of the case.

4. Carla gave Fred Florence her attorney the information he had requested.

5. If Phoebe seeks legal advice regarding the lawsuit she will be better prepared.

6. The cost of the various procedures were never explained.

7. We will however be responsible for paying the contingency fee for legal counsel.

8. Don't you want to ask your client Linda Rowan if she has any other pertinent information regarding the case.

9. When you have all the documentation to be keyed into the computer give it to our legal secretary Sarah Buck.

10. JENNIFER NELSON is the plaintiff in the case. (Sentence in a legal document.)

Determine the proper word division for the words below:

strained   stormy
enough   disturb

E Composition

1. Compose and key a paragraph applying the word mastery, word usage, spelling, and language skills you have studied.

2. Compose and key a second paragraph that explains how the terms *witness* and *testimony* are related.

3. Compose and key a third paragraph that explains some responsibilities of an attorney by using some of the Word Mastery terms. Submit all three paragraphs to your instructor.

F Research

1. Conduct research using the Internet, newspaper, and library or talk with individuals who are actually employed in the legal field to obtain information about the topics listed below. When searching online, go to the U.S. Bureau of Labor Statistics website at **www.bls.gov** and click on the **Publications** tab. Then click on the *Occupational Outlook Handbook* and **Index** links. Click on the first letter of the name of the field. (Example: Click on the letter *L* and scroll down the screen to find information on professions in the *law* or *legal* fields.) You can also do an online search of the name of the field/industry followed by the words *career* or *training*. (Example: *legal career* or *legal training*)

   - What are the employment opportunities for office workers in the legal field?

   - What are the advantages and/or disadvantages of employment in this field?

   - What skills or characteristics are necessary for someone who wants to work in this field?

   - What are the job titles or positions in this field?

   - What are the salary ranges for positions in this field?

   - What additional information did you learn during this research?

2. Compose and key paragraphs that address the questions above. Add a meaningful title. Include your name and the date. Proofread, edit, and revise the paragraphs to correct all grammar and spelling errors. Print the document. Proofread it again and make any final changes before submitting it to your instructor.

TRANSCRIPTION PREVIEW

In this chapter you will key five documents using three different forms. Two of the forms are preprinted and involve listening to dictation, keying information in the underlined spaces, and then removing the underlines. The Certificate of Notary form is not preprinted. You must key the entire form from the dictation given. Review the format below and on the next page to learn how to prepare the Certificate of Notary.

Certificate of Notary

- Use 1″ top and side margins and 11-point Calibri font.

- Key the heading *CERTIFICATE OF NOTARY* in uppercase. Select the heading and click on the Center command button.

- Tap ENTER twice after the heading and key the *STATE OF* line. Tab to the center point (3.25″) and key the right parenthesis.

- Tap ENTER once, tab to the center point, key the right parenthesis followed by two spaces, and key *ss*.

- Tap ENTER once and key the *COUNTY OF* line. Tab to the center point and key the right parenthesis.
- Tap ENTER twice to key the body of the form. Set a tab at 0.25″ and indent the first line of each paragraph.
- Tap ENTER twice after the body of the form. Tab to the center point to key the under-score to the right margin for the signature line.
- Tap ENTER once and tab to the center point. Key the last line of the form.

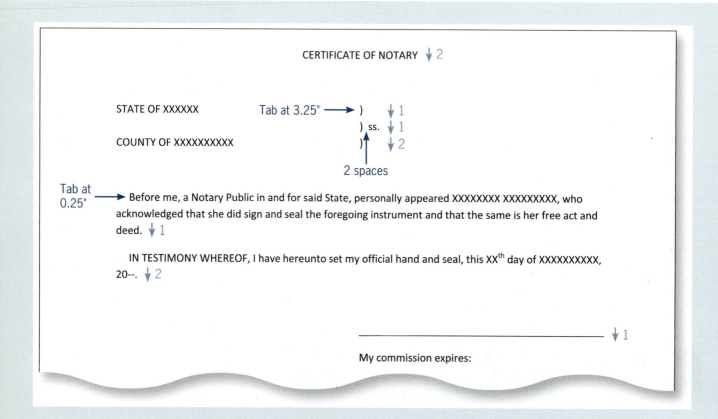

TRANSCRIPTION EXERCISES

1. Transcribe the Word Mastery terms from the Transcription CD.

2. Transcribe the five documents from the Transcription CD following the instructions below and using the current date unless another date is given.

   - Open Document 1 and use the Contingency Fee Agreement form. Key the variable information on the underlines in the document, and then remove the underlines.

   - Open Document 2 and use plain paper. Key the information for a Certificate of Notary.

- Open Document 3 and use the Probate Court form. Key the variable information on the underlines in the document, and then remove the underlines.

- Open Document 4 and use the Contingency Fee Agreement form. Key the variable information on the underlines in the document, and then remove the underlines.

- Open Document 5 and use the Probate Court form. Key the variable information on the underlines in the document, and then remove the underlines.

3. When you have transcribed a document using the file from the Transcription CD, remember to use the **Save As** feature and a distinctive name as the file name for each document.

4. Spell-check, proofread, and submit all five documents to your instructor for approval.

CHAPTER CHECKPOINTS

Place a check mark beside the objectives
you can meet after completing this chapter.

_____ I can define, spell, and use the Word Mastery terms in this chapter.

_____ I can use the commonly misused terms from the Word Usage section in this chapter.

_____ I can spell correctly the words in the Spelling section in this chapter.

_____ I can apply the rules for capitalization and word division presented in the Language Skills section in this chapter and other punctuation and grammar rules presented in earlier chapters.

_____ I can transcribe legal documents, including a Contingency Fee Agreement, a Certificate of Notary, and a Probate Court form, and proofread carefully.

Evaluation Form

Access the Evaluation Form from your Transcription CD. Complete it and submit it with your work. You may choose to either print the form and complete it or complete the form electronically.

© PaulPaladin/Shutterstock.com

Chapter 14

BILL OF SALE, COMPLAINT ON ACCOUNT, AND NOTICE OF GARNISHMENT

In Chapter 13 you began your study of the legal field. This chapter will include some additional legal documents for you to transcribe—a Bill of Sale, a Complaint on Account, and a Notice of Garnishment.

Since law is concerned with defining what is and what is not permissible in society, the language and the style of legal documents are quite formal. Care must be taken with all information presented in a legal context.

A Word Mastery Preview

Directions: Review the list of Word Mastery terms that will be used in the documents you will be transcribing. Learn the definition for each word and how to spell it correctly.

---

presents   *Definition:* term used to identify and refer to a document itself; that is, by the facts presented

Example: "By these presents" is an example of a traditional phrase that appears regularly in legal instruments.

---

complaint   *Definition:* a formal charge that a defendant has caused a plaintiff offense or injury

Example: Bailey's lawyer filed a complaint stating that Phil had taken the money.

---

account   *Definition:* a record of monetary transactions

Example: Every bank keeps an account of the money it takes from and lends to customers.

---

plaintiff   *Definition:* one who brings a legal action against a defendant

Example: Prospero and Caliban, Inc., was the plaintiff; and Ferdinand, the alleged trespasser on company property, was the defendant.

---

defendant   *Definition:* one against whom a legal action is brought by a plaintiff

Example: Ferdinand will be the defendant in a lawsuit if Prospero and Caliban, Inc., takes him to court for trespassing.

---

affidavit   *Definition:* a written or printed declaration sworn under oath to a person with authority to administer the oath

Example: Because she had witnessed the accident, Elena signed an affidavit in which she stated what she had seen.

---

order   *Definition:* something commanded to be done by a court of law

Example: The court order was that the defendant begin paying alimony.

---

garnishment   *Definition:* a legal notice that orders the attachment of a defendant's money or property to satisfy a debt

Example: Aneesha's lawyer requested the court to order the garnishment of her ex-husband's salary.

| garnishee | *Definition:* | the person or business whose money or property is being attached |
| | *Example:* | Daniel was the garnishee because he had refused to pay alimony. |

| attachment | *Definition:* | taking legal possession of a person or property |
| | *Example:* | The bank has a legal right to the attachment of Bernard's car because he failed to stay current on his payments. |

 **Word Usage**

Directions: Learn to spell and define these confusing words, which may occur within the documents you will be transcribing.

| adjoin | (verb) to be next to or near |
| adjourn | (verb) to end as in a trial or a meeting |

| altar | (noun) part of a church |
| alter | (verb) to change |

| cents | (noun) less than a dollar |
| sense | (noun) feeling; meaning |

| disburse | (verb) to pay out from a fund |
| disperse | (verb) to scatter |

| explicit | (adjective) easily understood |
| implicit | (adjective) implied or hidden |

| moral | (adjective) ethical; righteous |
| morale | (noun) a state of well-being |

their	(pronoun or adjective) belonging to them
there	(adverb) in that place
they're	(noun plus verb) the contraction of *they are*

 **Spelling**

Directions: Learn to spell these common words.

accumulate	friend	proceed
category	identity	quantity
chargeable	liaison	religious
desirable	mortgage	simultaneously
endeavor	possession	unanimous

D Language Skills

Directions: Enhance your language skills by reviewing basic grammar, punctuation, capitalization, number/figure style, abbreviation style, and word division rules. Study the rules and examples below.

Rule:	When keying monetary amounts in words within legal documents, begin each word with a capital letter followed by the monetary amount written in figures and enclosed in parentheses.
Examples:	• The defendant will pay One Thousand Five Hundred and Fifty-Five Dollars and Fifty-Five Cents ($1,555.55).
	• She will receive Five Thousand Dollars ($5,000) a month in alimony.
Rule:	When a word containing three or more syllables is to be divided at a one-letter syllable, divide after the syllable rather than before it.
Examples:	• maga-zine, not mag-azine
	• regu-lar, not reg-ular
Rule:	When two separately sounded vowels come together in a word, divide between the vowels.
Examples:	• situ-ation, not sit-uation or situa-tion
	• valu-able, not val-uable or valua-ble

Proofreading Tips

- Check to be sure all pages of your document are in the correct order and no page is missing.
- Check to be sure any enclosure or attachment mentioned in your document is enclosed or attached.

ENGLISH SKILLS EXERCISES

A Word Mastery

Directions: Apply what you learned in the English Skills Review. Choose the correct word in the following sentences from those found in the Word Mastery Preview.

1. The attorney made sure that he had filed the _____ against the defendant.

2. The _____ in the case is the one who begins the legal action.

3. Courtney's legal counsel advised her to sign the _____ that stated the information she knew.

4. If you do not pay your child support, a(n) _____ may be made on your salary.

5. Because a(n) _____ had been made on his vehicle, Ryan had no method of transportation.

6. Because he refused to pay child support, he became a(n) _____ so the money could be obtained.

7. Do you have a checking _____ with our local bank?

8. The plaintiff and the _____ did not look at each other during court.

9. Because of the court _____, Michael was required to perform several community service activities.

10. The term "By these _____" is used at the beginning of many legal documents.

B Word Usage

Directions: Choose the correct word in each of the following sentences.

1. If (their, there, they're) going to find a good attorney, they need to get their friends to give them suggestions rather than just looking in the phone book.

2. What was the (moral, morale) in the office after the staff found out Robert lost his job?

3. The paralegal was given (explicit, implicit) details that even a small child could follow to complete the task.

4. After entering the church, she felt compelled to kneel at the (altar, alter).

5. Because I wanted the new addition to (adjoin, adjourn) the original building and be aligned perfectly, I insisted the architect check the specifications for the fifth time.

6. When you think you can make (cents, sense) of what the client is ranting about, tell the attorney what she wants.

7. Why did you (disburse, disperse) the funds when you did not have authorization to do so?

8. If the meeting goes more than two hours, his legal secretary was told to remind him discreetly to (adjoin, adjourn) the session.

9. (Their, There, They're) attorney did not feel they could win the appeal.

10. You cannot (altar, alter) the document after it has been signed.

C Spelling

Directions: Choose the correct spelling in each of the following sentences.

1. If you can (accumulate, acummulate) enough money for the down payment, your (morgage, mortgage) will probably be approved.

2. Because of her (religious, religous) beliefs, the jury was not (unanemas, unanimous) in their decision.

3. (Simultaneously, Simultaniously) both attorneys said they objected to the comment made on the witness stand.

4. What (category, catagory) do you think is the most (desirable, disireable) to choose?

5. I will (procede, proceed) to (endeavor, endevor) to obtain the information from the witness.

6. Because Patty was her (freind, friend), she came forward and admitted her guilt.

7. Do you prefer (quantity, quantaty) or quality when purchasing clothing for work?

8. Betty Jean's (identity, identaty) was stolen by someone from another state.

9. My (liaison, liasion) did not relay the information to me.

10. Some of the expenses could not be (chargeable, chargable) to the company.

D Language Skills

Directions: Use proofreaders' marks to make corrections in the following sentences. Write "Correct" by the sentence if no corrections are needed. Some of these sentences include a review of language skills presented in previous chapters. You may want to refer to the reference manual in the back of this text-workbook for a review before completing these examples.

1. The plaintiff will receive One hundred forty dollars and fifty cents ($140.50). (Written in a legal document.)

2. We hope to visit Orlando, Florida on our vacation next year.

3. Therefore you must submit the information to the attorney immediately.

4. The legal office professional typed wills bills of sales and affidavits.

5. The total amount of the judgment was Three thousand five hundred dollars and forty cents ($3,500.40). (Written in a legal document.)

6. Is his law firm in Greenville South Carolina Columbia South Carolina or Charleston South Carolina.

7. Of course I hope to obtain a job as a paralegal when I graduate.

8. The amount to be awarded to the plaintiff will be three hundred dollars. (Written in a legal document).

9. Rebecca, Susan and Lisa worked in the law firm on Main Street.

10. Nevertheless the client felt his attorney did not handle the case well.

Determine the proper word division for the words below:

minimum   graduation

medicine   ravioli

E Composition

1. Compose and key a paragraph applying the word mastery, word usage, spelling, and language skills you have studied.

2. Compose and key a second paragraph that describes the difference between a *defendant* and a *plaintiff.*

3. Compose and key a third paragraph that explains the terms *garnishee* and *garnishment.* Submit all three paragraphs to your instructor.

F Research

1. Locate five recent articles from newspapers, magazines, the library, or the Internet that relate to legal ethics, legal cases, legal documents, legal terminology, or the legal profession.

2. List the source and date of each article and summarize it in paragraph format. Include your name and the date. Proofread, edit, and revise the paragraphs to correct all grammar and spelling errors. Print the documents. Proofread them again and make any final changes before submitting them to your instructor.

TRANSCRIPTION PREVIEW

In this chapter you will key five documents using three forms. Two of the forms are preprinted and involve listening to dictation, keying information in the underlined spaces, and then removing the underlines. The Bill of Sale form is not preprinted. You must key the entire form from the dictation given. Review the format below and on the next page to learn how to prepare the Bill of Sale.

Bill of Sale

- Use 1″ top and side margins and 11-point Calibri font.
- Key the heading BILL OF SALE in uppercase. Select the heading and click on the Center command button.
- Tap ENTER once after the heading to begin keying the body. Set a tab at 0.25″ and indent the first line of each paragraph.
- Tap ENTER twice after the body of the form. Tab to the center point (3.25″) to key the underscore to the right margin for the signature line. Key the seller's name directly below the signature line.
- Tap ENTER twice after the seller's name to begin keying the rest of the form, which is a Certificate of Notary. See the directions for keying a Certificate of Notary in Chapter 13.

BILL OF SALE ↓ 1

Tab at → 0.25"

KNOW ALL MEN BY THESE PRESENTS that XXXXXXXXXXX, XXXXXXXXXXXXXXXXXX, herein referred to as Seller, in consideration of XXXXXXXXXXX ($XXXXXX), to Seller paid by XXXXXXXXXXXXXXXXXXX, XXXXXXXXXXXXXXXXXXXXXXXXXXXXXXXXX, herein referred to as Buyer. The receipt whereof is hereby acknowledged, does hereby grant, bargain, sell, and convey to the said Buyer, her executors, administrators, and assigns, the following described personal property, to wit: one (1) XXXXXXXX, one (1) XXXXXXXXXXXXXXXXXXXXXXXXXXXXXXXXXXX four (4) XXXXXXXXXXXXXXXXXXXXXXXXXXXX, and one (1) XXXXXXXXXXXXXXXXXXXXXXXXXXXXXXXXXXXXXXXXXXX, to have and to hold the same unto the said Buyer, her executors, administrators, and assigns forever. ↓ 1

And the said Seller, for himself and for his heirs, executors, and administrators, does hereby covenant with the said Buyer, her executors, administrators, and assigns, that Seller is the true and lawful owner of the said described property hereby sold, and has full power to sell and convey the same; that the title, so conveyed, is clear, free, and unencumbered; and further that Seller will warrant and defend the same against all claims or demands of all persons whomsoever. ↓ 1

IN WITNESS WHEREOF, the said Seller has hereunto set his hand and seal this XXth day of XXXXXXXX, 20--. ↓ 2

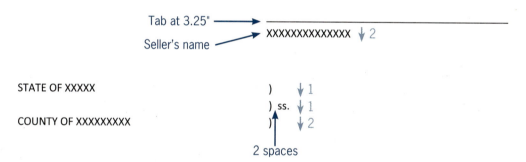

Tab at 3.25" → _____

Seller's name → XXXXXXXXXXXXXX ↓ 2

STATE OF XXXXX) ↓ 1

) ss. ↓ 1

COUNTY OF XXXXXXXXX) ↓ 2

2 spaces

Before me, a Notary Public in and for said State, personally appeared XXXXXXXXXXXXXXXX, who acknowledged that he did sign and seal the foregoing instrument and that the same is his free act and deed. ↓ 1

IN TESTIMONY WHEREOF, I have hereunto set my official hand and seal, this XXth day of XXXXXXXXXXX, 20--. ↓ 2

_____ ↓ 1

My commission expires:

1. Transcribe the Word Mastery terms from the Transcription CD.

2. Transcribe the five documents from the Transcription CD following the instructions below and using the current date unless another date is given.

   • Open Document 1, use plain paper, and key a Bill of Sale.

   • Open Document 2 and use the Complaint on Account form. Key the variable information on the underlines in the document, and then remove the underlines.

   • Open Document 3 and use the Affidavit, Order, and Notice of Garnishment form. Key the variable information on the underlines in the document, and then remove the underlines.

   • Open Document 4 and use the Complaint on Account form. Key the variable information on the underlines in the document, and then remove the underlines.

   • Open Document 5 and use the Affidavit, Order, and Notice of Garnishment form. Key the variable information on the underlines in the document, and then remove the underlines.

3. When you have transcribed a document using the file from the Transcription CD, remember to use the *Save As* feature and a distinctive name as the file name for each document.

4. Spell-check, proofread, and submit all five documents to your instructor for approval.

CHAPTER CHECKPOINTS

Place a check mark beside the objectives
you can meet after completing this chapter.

_____ I can define, spell, and use the Word Mastery terms in this chapter.

_____ I can use the commonly misused terms from the Word Usage section in
this chapter.

_____ I can spell correctly the words in the Spelling section in this chapter.

_____ I can apply the rules for number/figure style and word division presented
in the Language Skills section in this chapter and other punctuation and
grammar rules presented in earlier chapters.

_____ I can transcribe legal documents, including a Bill of Sale, a Complaint on
Account form, and a Notice of Garnishment, and proofread carefully.

✳ Evaluation Form

Access the Evaluation Form from your Transcription CD. Complete it and
submit it with your work. You may choose to either print the form and
complete it or complete the form electronically.

© Monkey Business Images/Shutterstock.com

Chapter 15

PETITION FOR DISSOLUTION OF MARRIAGE, BILLING STATEMENTS, AND PARTNERSHIP AGREEMENT

The documents in this chapter pertain to marriage and partnerships and also include billing statements. In the majority of legal offices, clients are usually billed based on the amount of time the attorney spends working on the particular case.

ENGLISH SKILLS REVIEW

A Word Mastery Preview

Directions: Review the list of Word Mastery terms that will be used in the documents you will be transcribing. Learn the definition for each word and how to spell it correctly.

petition	*Definition:*	a written application to the court for action on a legal matter
	Example:	Wes and Angie's attorney filed a petition for them to adopt a baby.
dissolution	*Definition:*	the separation or breaking of a legal bond or tie
	Example:	Dion and Jane were granted a dissolution of their marriage.
filing	*Definition:*	placing papers with the clerk of a court
	Example:	Joanne is filing to start her business under the name "Stylus, Inc.," but she must wait to see if the name is already being used.
petitioners	*Definition:*	the people who file a legal request
	Example:	The petitioners filed a lawsuit in probate court.
residents	*Definition:*	those who live in a certain place
	Example:	Janis and Hunter have been residents of this apartment building for many years.
issue	*Definition:*	offspring; children
	Example:	When someone dies without issue, that person will often leave his or her estate to relatives or close friends.
amendments	*Definition:*	corrections or changes
	Example:	When she reread her essay, Myrna made amendments to one of her reference notes.
decree	*Definition:*	an order or a decision issued by a legal authority
	Example:	The judge's decree stated that Rita and Raoul's marriage was officially dissolved.
statement	*Definition:*	a report of money owed for services performed
	Example:	Bridget prepared the client's statement for last month's charges.

| retainer | *Definition:* the fee paid to an attorney for hiring the attorney on an as-needed basis |
| | *Example:* Our company has an attorney on retainer who charges for every phone call we make to her. |

B Word Usage

Directions: Learn to spell and define these confusing words, which may occur within the documents you will be transcribing.

| bare | (adjective or verb) naked; to confess |
| bear | (noun or verb) an animal; to carry |

| credible | (adjective) believable |
| creditable | (adjective) meritorious or deserving of praise |

| device | (noun) a mechanical invention |
| devise | (verb) to plan, to contrive, or to bequest real property by a will |

| holy | (adjective) sacred |
| wholly | (adjective) entirely |

| marital | (adjective) wedded; nuptial |
| martial | (adjective) relating to military life |

| peace | (noun) calm |
| piece | (verb or noun) to join together; a part or an artistic work |

steal	(verb) embezzle; take
steel	(noun) metal
still	(adjective or verb) motionless; calm

C Spelling

Directions: Learn to spell these common words.

appreciate	caught	hypocrite
average	concede	interpret
basically	defiant	likable
brilliant	expect	niece
burglar	harassment	publicly

D Language Skills

Directions: Enhance your language skills by reviewing basic grammar, punctuation, capitalization, number/figure style, abbreviation style, and word division rules. Study the rules and examples below.

Rule: Use the abbreviation *Re:* in legal letters to represent *regarding* or *subject*. Note: In legal documents, the *Re:* line is not necessarily keyed below the salutation of a letter as is the subject line in regular business correspondence.

Examples:
- Re: Dissolution of Marriage (subject line within a legal letter)
- Re: Partnership Agreement (subject line within a legal letter)

Rule: If there are double consonants in a base word (a word without a prefix or a suffix), divide the word between the double consonants.

Examples:
- recom-mend
- com-ment

Rule: When a suffix is added to a word that ends in double consonants, divide the word after the double consonants if there is a syllable break between the double consonants and the suffix.

Examples:
- fill-ing
- kissed (even though the word ends in double consonants before the suffix is added, it cannot be divided because it is a one-syllable word)

Rule: If a final consonant is doubled when a suffix is added to a word, divide the word between the double consonants if there is a syllable break between the double consonants and the suffix.

Examples:
- refer-ring
- oc-curred (you cannot divide *occurred* between the double *r* before the suffix *ed* because there is not a syllable break at this point)

Proofreading Tips

- If you key a list or steps that one should take to accomplish a task or procedure, ask someone who is not familiar with the task or procedure to read what you have keyed to see if she or he would be able to perform the task or procedure based on the list or steps stated.

- If you key directions to a location, ask someone who is not familiar with that location to read what you have keyed to see if he or she would be able to find the location based on the directions stated. In the example given below, is the individual to turn right or left at the intersection?

  When you come to the intersection of Main Street and Elm Street, turn and my office will be two blocks on your left.

ENGLISH SKILLS EXERCISES

A Word Mastery

Directions: Apply what you learned in the English Skills Review. Choose the correct word in the following sentences from those found in the Word Mastery Preview.

1. Although they had been partners for years, the attorneys filed a(n) _____ to end the partnership.

2. The _____ of the house were not home.

3. Several _____ had to be made to the proposal before it was presented to the Board of Directors.

4. Jackson never received his monthly _____ from the company.

5. Because the attorney was on _____, the client could call him to discuss legal issues at any time.

6. The young couple plan on _____ for divorce within the next week.

7. Thelma and Louise were the _____ who filed the lawsuit against their employers.

8. Gabriella filed a(n) _____ to the court regarding the changing of her name.

9. The judge's _____ will be the final decision regarding the case.

10. Because Aunt Tilley died without _____, she left her entire estate to her niece, Katie.

B Word Usage

Directions: Choose the correct word in each of the following sentences.

1. The attorney was not sure if the witness would be (credible, creditable) enough for the jury to believe what he said on the stand.

2. Although Marianna was a strong individual, she did not think she could (bare, bear) to recount all the details regarding the robbery.

3. What type of (device, devise) did you invent?

4. When you need some (peace, piece) and quiet, you need to remove yourself from the task and take a break.

5. His father used to work in the (steal, steel, still) industry years ago.

6. Many people do not consider their marriage vows to be (holy, wholly).

7. If you (device, devise) a plan that you think will work, let the entire legal team know.

8. Everyone knows that you should not (steal, steel, still) from others.

9. Because they were having (marital, martial) problems, the young couple decided to seek a good marriage counselor rather than pursue a divorce.

10. Let's see if we can (peace, piece) together what took place the night of the crime.

C Spelling

Directions: Choose the correct spelling in each of the following sentences.

1. We certainly (appreciate, appreseate) your (publically, publicly) stating that the mayor was not involved in the embezzlement.

2. Although her parents thought she was an (avarage, average) student, they did not realize how (likable, likeable) she was.

3. (Basically, Basiclly) Elaine did not (expect, exspect) her attorney to win her appeal.

4. Unfortunately, my (neice, niece) was so (defiant, difiant) her parents had to ask her to leave home.

5. Be sure you are careful about comments you make because you don't want someone to claim you are guilty of (harassment, harrasment).

6. Although he never thought he would be (caught, caugt), the (burglar, burgler) was apprehended within three hours.

7. Since his SAT scores were so high, he told all his classmates that he was (brilliant, brillent).

8. People said Reshita was a (hypocrit, hypocrite) because she spoke out against the dangers of smoking; however, she owned stock in a major tobacco company.

9. If you try to (interpret, interprete) what you think he meant instead of what he actually said, you will never be correct.

10. I will (concede, conceed) to some of your demands if you will agree to meet some of mine.

D Language Skills

Directions: Use proofreaders' marks to make corrections in the following sentences. Write "Correct" by the sentence if no corrections are needed. Some of these sentences include a review of language skills presented in previous chapters. You may want to refer to the reference manual in the back of this text-workbook for a review before completing these examples.

1. The intelligent young attorney approached the judges bench.

2. We need to decide our law firms long range goals.

3. She keyed all of the legal documents for the day and she proceeded to file all of the material that needed to be filed.

4. Several attorneys desks needed to be moved into the next office.

5. We wanted the well known author to sign his book for us.

6. Because an attractive well dressed man was sitting behind the desk in the law office the clients assumed he was their attorney.

7. The paralegals were researching information the attorneys needed and they discovered some interesting facts.

8. Don't you want to contact a well educated attorney to handle the case for you.

9. The legal assistants notes were nowhere to be found even though she looked in several locations.

10. Since you have taken several legal courses and clerical courses finding a well paying rewarding position should not be difficult.

Determine the proper word division for the words below:

slipping	callers
embarrass	occurrence

E Composition

1. Compose and key a paragraph applying the word mastery, word usage, spelling, and language skills you have studied.

2. Compose and key a second paragraph that describes the types of service someone might need from an attorney.

3. Compose and key a third paragraph about an advertisement you have seen on television for a local attorney in your area. Submit all three paragraphs to your instructor.

F Research

1. Locate five recent articles from newspapers, magazines, the library, or the Internet that relate to legal ethics, legal cases, legal documents, legal terminology, or the legal profession that you did not use in previous chapters.

2. List the source and date of each article and summarize it in paragraph format. Include your name and the date. Proofread, edit, and revise the paragraphs to correct all grammar and spelling errors. Print the documents. Proofread them again and make any final changes before submitting them to your instructor.

TRANSCRIPTION PREVIEW

In this chapter you will key five documents using letterhead and three forms. Two forms are preprinted and involve listening to dictation, keying information in the underlined spaces, and then removing the underlines. The Petition for Dissolution of Marriage form is partially preprinted. You must key additional text to complete the form. Review the format below and on the next page to learn how to prepare the Petition for Dissolution of Marriage.

Petition for Dissolution of Marriage

- Use 1" top and side margins and 10-point Calibri font.

- Tap ENTER once between each enumerated item.

- Tap ENTER once after the last enumerated item. Key the last paragraph of the form.

- Tap ENTER once after the last paragraph. Tab to the center point (3.25") and key the complimentary closing line (*Respectfully submitted*).

- Tap ENTER three times after the complimentary closing. Tab to the center point and key the underscore to the right margin for the signature line.

- Key the attorney's name directly below the signature line.

- Key the petitioner's name directly below the *Attorney for Petitioner* line.

- Key the attorney's address and phone number directly below the petitioner's name.

- Tap ENTER three times after the attorney's phone number. Tab to the center point and key the underscore to the right margin for the first petitioner's signature line. Then key the petitioner's name directly below the signature line. Repeat these steps for the second petitioner. (Note: These lines may appear on the second page of the form if there are several enumerated items.)

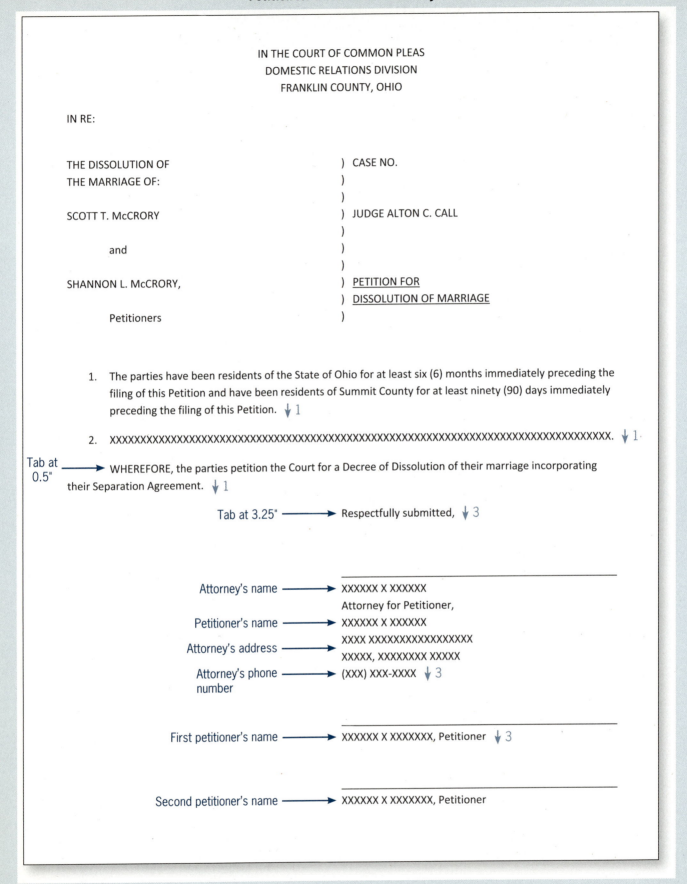

IN THE COURT OF COMMON PLEAS
DOMESTIC RELATIONS DIVISION
FRANKLIN COUNTY, OHIO

IN RE:

THE DISSOLUTION OF   ) CASE NO.
THE MARRIAGE OF:)
)
SCOTT T. McCRORY   ) JUDGE ALTON C. CALL
)
        and   )
)
SHANNON L. McCRORY,   ) PETITION FOR
) DISSOLUTION OF MARRIAGE
        Petitioners   )

1. The parties have been residents of the State of Ohio for at least six (6) months immediately preceding the filing of this Petition and have been residents of Summit County for at least ninety (90) days immediately preceding the filing of this Petition. ↓ 1

2. XXXXXXXXXXXXXXXXXXXXXXXXXXXXXXXXXXXXXXXXXXXXXXXXXXXXXXXXXXXXXXXXXXXXXXXXXXXXXXXXXXXXXX. ↓ 1

Tab at 0.5" ——→ WHEREFORE, the parties petition the Court for a Decree of Dissolution of their marriage incorporating their Separation Agreement. ↓ 1

Tab at 3.25" ——→ Respectfully submitted, ↓ 3

                                            _____
Attorney's name ——————→ XXXXXX X XXXXXX
                                            Attorney for Petitioner,
Petitioner's name ——————→ XXXXXX X XXXXXX
                                            XXXX XXXXXXXXXXXXXXXXX
Attorney's address ——————→ XXXXX, XXXXXXXX XXXXX
Attorney's phone ——————→ (XXX) XXX-XXXX ↓ 3
number

                                            _____
First petitioner's name ——————→ XXXXXX X XXXXXXX, Petitioner ↓ 3

                                            _____
Second petitioner's name ——————→ XXXXXX X XXXXXXX, Petitioner

NOTE: The top portion above the enumerated items in the Petition for Dissolution of Marriage is preprinted. Additional text will be dictated and should be formatted as shown above.

1. Transcribe the Word Mastery terms from the Transcription CD.

2. Transcribe the five documents from the Transcription CD following the instructions below and using the current date.

   • Open Document 1 and use the letterhead for the Simonson law firm. Key this document in block letter style with mixed punctuation.

   • Open Document 2 and use the Petition for Dissolution of Marriage form. Key the additional information to be included on the form as dictated.

   • Open Document 3 and use the Billing Statement form. Key the variable information on the underlines, and then remove them.

   • Open Document 4 and use the Partnership Agreement form. Key the variable information on the underlines, and then remove them.

   • Open Document 5 and use the Billing Statement form. Key the variable information on the underlines, and then remove them.

2. When you have transcribed a document using the file from the Transcription CD, remember to use the **Save As** feature and a distinctive file name.

3. Spell-check, proofread, and submit all five documents to your instructor.

CHAPTER CHECKPOINTS

Place a check mark beside the objectives you can meet after completing this chapter.

_____ I can define, spell, and use the Word Mastery terms in this chapter.

_____ I can use the commonly misused terms from the Word Usage section in this chapter.

_____ I can spell correctly the words in the Spelling section in this chapter.

_____ I can apply the rules for abbreviations and word division presented in the Language Skills section in this chapter and other punctuation and grammar rules presented in earlier chapters.

_____ I can transcribe legal documents, including a Petition for Dissolution of Marriage, a Billing Statement, and a Partnership Agreement, and proofread carefully.

✳ Evaluation Form

Access the Evaluation Form from your Transcription CD. Complete it and submit it with your work. You may choose to either print the form and complete it or complete the form electronically.

© Lane V. Erickson/Shutterstock.com

Chapter 16

ESTATE AND TAX MATTERS, LAST WILL AND TESTAMENT, AND POWER OF ATTORNEY

In this last chapter about the legal field, emphasis will be placed on documents for handling matters relating to the end of life, such as an individual's estate.

Word Mastery Preview

Directions: Review the list of Word Mastery terms that will be used in the documents you will be transcribing. Learn the definition for each word and how to spell it correctly.

| tax | *Definition:* | payment required from a person, business, or property owner to support and maintain a government |
| | *Example:* | My parents must pay a property tax on the land they own. |

| status | *Definition:* | the condition, state, or rank of someone or something |
| | *Example:* | Mike's status among his colleagues was elevated when they learned that he had been promoted. |

| citizen | *Definition:* | a person owing loyalty to and entitled to the protection of a government, either by birthright or by having been given such a right by that government |
| | *Example:* | Raymond, who was born in Bathurst, is a Gambian citizen. |

| fiscal | *Definition:* | having to do with finances, especially those of a government |
| | *Example:* | The United States' fiscal policies changed dramatically during the Great Depression of the 1930s. |

| evasion | *Definition:* | the act of avoiding or eluding |
| | *Example:* | Because he did not know the answer to the instructor's question, the student talked in generalities in an attempt at evasion. |

| compensation | *Definition:* | payment |
| | *Example:* | In return for compensation, Lawrence is to work efficiently 40 hours each week. |

| substantiate | *Definition:* | to verify or establish something as true |
| | *Example:* | The attorney learned that her client had not been honest and could not substantiate what she had claimed. |

| executor | *Definition:* | one named by the maker of a will to fulfill the terms of the will after the maker's death |
| | *Example:* | Kim received her parent's home and property through her Uncle Brad, who had been named executor of the estate. |

| estate | *Definition:* | any kind of property that an individual owns and can dispose of in a will |
| | *Example:* | The millionaire's estate was divided equally among his children. |

| rights | *Definition:* | proper and lawful claim to or interest in something |
| | *Example:* | Maria just sold the rights to her first song to a recording company. |

| contract | *Definition:* | a legally binding, formal agreement between two or more parties |
| | *Example:* | Before her first book was published, Benedicta signed a contract in which she agreed to the terms of the sale, distribution of the books, and payment of royalties. |

| carry-ons | *Definition:* | series of books continuing the story of the same character |
| | *Example:* | After reading the first book, I was anxious to read the other carry-ons that the author had written about the heroine. |

| pastiches | *Definition:* | a piece of literary, artistic, musical, or architectural work that imitates the style of previous work |
| | *Example:* | The author's pastiches were best sellers because readers had enjoyed his previous books. |

B Word Usage

Directions: Learn to spell and define these confusing words, which may occur within the documents you will be transcribing.

| liable | (adjective) legally responsible |
| libel | (verb) to make a false written statement |

| packed | (adjective or verb) crowded; past tense of *to pack* |
| pact | (noun) an agreement |

| partition | (noun) division |
| petition | (noun) prayer or formal written request |

| peruse | (verb) to look over in an attentive manner |
| pursue | (verb) to chase |

right	(adjective or noun) correct; privilege
rite	(noun) a ceremony
write	(verb) to inscribe

tort	(noun) criminal wrongdoing
torte	(noun) a type of cake

waiver	(noun) the giving up of a claim
waver	(verb) to hesitate

C Spelling

Directions: Learn to spell these common words.

acquit	inaugurate	subtle
amend	lying	succeed
colleague	prejudice	surveys
gratuity	readable	tremendous
ignorance	reference	voluntarily

D Language Skills

Directions: Enhance your language skills by reviewing basic grammar, punctuation, capitalization, number/figure style, abbreviation style, and word division rules. Study the rules and examples below.

Rule: Divide a compound word between the elements of the compound word.

Examples:
- eye-witness not eyewit-ness
- head-master not headmas-ter

Rule: Divide hyphenated words only at the hyphen.

Examples:
- self-confident not self-confi-dent
- self-conscious not self-con-scious

Rule: When dividing a date between lines, divide between the day of the month and the year. A hyphen is not used in this division.

Examples:
- August 13,
  2010

  not

  August
  13, 2010

Proofreading Tips

- When proofreading a document on your computer screen, focus on viewing just a line at a time and use the downward directional arrow to access each successive line.

- If you are proofreading a printed document, focus on viewing just a line at a time by using some type of device (another sheet of paper or a ruler) to keep your eye focused on one line at a time.

Rule: When dividing a name between lines, divide between the middle initial and the surname. If no middle initial is given, divide between the first name and surname. Do not separate titles from the first name or from the surname if the first name is not given. Hyphens are not used in this division.

Examples:

- Mary E. Cohen
- Mrs. Mary Cohen
- Dr. Gonzales

not

Mary E. Cohen

not

Mrs. Mary Cohen

not

Dr. Gonzales

Rule: If it is necessary to separate an address between lines, keep together the number and street name and keep together the state and ZIP code. You may separate an address between the street name and city name or between the city name and the state name. Hyphens are not used in this division.

Examples:

- 123 Rowan Street
  Nashville, TN 37203-6109

or

123 Rowan Street
Nashville,
TN 37203-6109

not

123
Rowan Street
Nashville, TN
37203-6109

ENGLISH SKILLS EXERCISES

A Word Mastery

Directions: Apply what you learned in the English Skills Review. Choose the correct word in the following sentences from those found in the Word Mastery Preview.

1. Have you paid the sales _____ on the car you bought?

2. Although Els was born in Holland, she is now a(n) _____ of the United States.

3. Will I receive the _____ we agreed upon for my services?

4. Trevor was the _____ of his wife's estate.

5. You will have to relinquish all _____ to the property when you sell it to someone else.

6. When they formed their partnership, all parties signed a(n) _____ listing the terms of their agreement.

7. Roxanne's attorney suggested she make plans regarding her _____ to ensure that her assets would be distributed as she wanted when she died.

8. You will need to _____ your whereabouts during the time of the crime.

9. The _____ year that many companies use to report their income and expenses does not correspond with the calendar year.

10. Tax _____ may occur; however, one may eventually be caught and will face stern penalties.

B Word Usage

Directions: Choose the correct word in each of the following sentences.

1. Would you like to (peruse, pursue) the legal briefs?

2. Because not everyone wanted the big super store to build in the neighborhood, Nancy and Grayson were able to get 126 people to sign the (partition, petition).

3. I want to be very careful driving my friend's car because I do not want to be (liable, libel) should I have an accident.

4. The courtroom was so (packed, pact) that there was standing room only.

5. As I began to (right, rite, write) in my journal, I reflected on the wonderful afternoon our family had at the park.

6. When you decide what you think is the best decision, don't (waiver, waver).

7. The waiter asked if we wanted to have the apple (tort, torte) for dessert.

8. Several high school students made a (packed, pact) that they would not drink and drive or use their cell phones while driving.

9. If you have a goal set in your mind, don't let anything stop you as you (peruse, pursue) your dreams.

10. What (right, rite, write) do you have to tell me how to live my life?

C Spelling

Directions: Choose the correct spelling in each of the following sentences.

1. Belinda felt she needed to (amend, ammend) the document so it would be more (readable, readible) for her young client.

2. After her (coleague, colleague) offered to pay for both their meals, Suzette felt she needed to pay the (gratuety, gratuity).

Spelling (continued)

3. Several of her customers (voluntarily, voluntarilly) completed the (survays, surveys) at the local boutique.

4. Just because I can't tolerate (lieing, lying) from anyone doesn't make me (prejudice, prejuduss).

5. Mr. Johnson, the principal, will (inaugerate, inaugurate) the student body officers tomorrow.

6. As (pecular, peculiar) as it may seem, Rubiana left (subtle, suttle) reminders all around her home to remind her of things she needed to do.

7. If you really want to (succede, succeed), try and try again until you reach your goal.

8. When you want to list someone as a (referance, reference) on your resume, be sure you obtain permission from the person first.

9. Have you ever heard the expression that (ignerance, ignorance) is bliss?

10. It is going to take a (tremendous, tremmendous) effort by our entire legal team to win the case.

D Language Skills

Directions: Use proofreaders' marks to make corrections in the following sentences. Write "Correct" by the sentence if no corrections are needed. Some of these sentences include a review of language skills presented in previous chapters. You may want to refer to the reference manual in the back of this text-workbook for a review before completing these examples.

1. Be sure to consult your attorney Roddy before you go to court.

2. In August we hope our family can all join us for our family vacation.

3. The paraprofessionals and office staff were all at lunch therefore no one could assist the attorney with the paperwork for the case.

4. Some students in the class indicated they wanted to pursue a career in the legal field other students stated they preferred the medical field.

5. The stress of the day of course took its toll on everyone in the office but they all knew they had to complete the report make copies and collate the material before the meeting.

6. Of course everyone wants to do his/her best but this does not mean everything will be done to perfection.

7. Her daughter Karen decided to pursue a paralegal career, her daughter Gracie decided to pursue a legal secretary career.

8. In the afternoon the attorney preferred to have no appointments scheduled after 4 p.m.

9. At the very last moment we realized we had not scheduled the conference room for the meeting.

10. We cannot afford to hire any more full time staff however we can hire some part time employees temporarily.

Determine the proper place to divide the words or phrases below.

checkbook	January 31, 2011
self-fulfilled	Mr. Juan Diego

E Composition

1. Compose and key a paragraph applying the word mastery, word usage, spelling, and language skills you have studied.

2. Compose and key a second paragraph that describes a time you received compensation for something you did.

3. Compose and key a third paragraph that describes a time you or someone you know practiced some type of evasion. Submit all three paragraphs to your instructor.

F Research

1. Locate five recent articles from newspapers, magazines, the library, or the Internet that relate to legal ethics, legal cases, legal documents, legal terminology, or the legal profession that you did not use in previous chapters.

2. List the source and date of each article and summarize it in paragraph format. Include your name and the date. Proofread, edit, and revise the paragraphs to correct all grammar and spelling errors. Print the documents. Proofread them again and make any final changes before submitting them to your instructor.

TRANSCRIPTION PREVIEW

In this chapter you will key five documents using letterhead, a form letter, and two legal forms. The form letter and the two legal forms are preprinted and involve listening to dictation, keying information in the underlined spaces, and then removing the underlines. One of the preprinted forms, the Durable Power of Attorney, will involve keying additional text to complete the form. Review the format shown on the following pages to become familiar with the Durable Power of Attorney.

STATE OF_____)

COUNTY OF _____)

DURABLE POWER OF ATTORNEY

      KNOW ALL MEN BY THESE PRESENTS that I, _____, of the County of _____, State of _____, do hereby constitute and appoint _____, of _____, _____, as my true and lawful Attorney to set in, manage, and conduct all my estate and all my affairs for me in my name, place and stead, for my use and benefit, and as my act and deed, to do and execute, or to concur with persons jointly interested with myself therein in the doing and executing, with the full power to have and to exercise the following powers in a fiduciary capacity, without authorization of any court and in addition to any other rights, powers, or authority granted by statue or general rule of law.

REVOCATION OF PRIOR POWERS

      I hereby revoke all powers of attorney, general and/or limited, heretofore granted by me as principal and terminate all agency relationship created thereunder, including those of all successor Agents named therein, if any, except that powers granted by me on forms provided by financial institutions granting the right to write checks or deposit funds to and withdraw funds from accounts to which I am a signatory or granting access to a safe deposit box and any health care power of attorney that I may have executed shall not be revoked, but shall continue in full force and effect.

Tab at 0.5"

POWERS IN GENERAL

1.   To buy, sell or exchange, mortgage, convey, lease, contract with respect to, or option any property of mine, whether real, personal or mixed, which I may now own or hereafter acquire, specifically including, but not limited to real estate, stocks, bonds or other securities, upon such terms and conditions (including credit) as my Attorney shall deem best in the Attorney's absolute discretion; ↓ 1

2.   To sign checks withdrawing or transferring funds or money from any financial institutions, including banks or savings and loan associations, in which money may be deposited in my name alone or in join name with someone else, and to accept, sign, seal, negotiate, acknowledge, collect and endorse any checks, drafts or other instruments for the payment of money, including Social Security and other United States Government checks and any state government checks; ↓ 1

3.   To borrow money and execute notes or other instruments securing the repayment and to pledge as security therefore any stocks, bonds, securities, or property which I may own, and/or to mortgage any real or personal property which I may own, in order to secure said loan; ↓ 1

GENERAL PROVISIONS

1.   **AND I**, the said _____, do hereby ratify and confirm all acts of my Attorney, and do declare that all acts and deeds performed under this instrument shall have the same full force

1

(Continued)

NOTE: The Durable Power of Attorney form is preprinted. Key the information dictated in the underlined spaces and then remove the underlines. Additional enumerated items will be dictated and should be formatted as shown above.

and effect as if performed and signed by me in person, and this instrument shall be effective until revoked in writing and filed in the public records of the county first set out above or shall cease by operation of law and shall be binding upon myself, my heirs, devisees, legatees, beneficiaries, legal representatives, and assigns.

2. This instrument is to be construed and interpreted as a general Power of Attorney without limitation or reservation. The enumeration of specific items, rights, acts, or powers herein is not intended to, nor does it limit or restrict, and is not to be construed or interpreted as limiting or restricting, the general powers herein granted to my said Attorney.

3. This Power of Attorney shall not be affected by the physical disability or mental incompetence of the principal which renders the principal incapable of managing his/her own estate.

4. My Attorney may resign at any time by giving a written resignation to me and filing a copy of said resignation in the public records of the county first set out above.

5. My Attorney may be removed by me or this Power of Attorney may be amended or revoked by me by my filing a written instrument in the public records of the county first set above.

6. My Attorney shall not be required to file an accounting or inventory with any Probate Court, but shall maintain accurate records and/or books of account in order to account to me or my heirs or my personal representatives. I direct that no surety bond or security shall be required of my Attorney, even after my mental disability.

IN WITNESS WHEREOF, I have hereunto set my hand and seal this the _____ day of _____, _____.

_____

_____, PRINCIPAL

SIGNED, SEALED, PUBLISHED, AND DECLARED by the principal, _____, as and for her Power of Attorney in the presence of us, who at the principal's request, in the presence of the principal and in the presence of each other, have hereto subscribed our names as witnesses hereto.

_____ of _____, _____, _____

_____ of _____ , _____, _____

2

(Continued)

STATE OF _____)

_____)

COUNTY OF _____)

      PERSONALLY appeared before me the below signed witness and made oath that (s)he saw the within _____, sign, seal, and her act and deed deliver the within Power of Attorney and that (s)he with the other witness witnessed the execution thereof.

_____
                              (Witness)

SWORN to before me this _____

Day of _____, ____

_____

Notary Public for _____

My Commission Expires: _____

3

TRANSCRIPTION EXERCISES

1. Transcribe the Word Mastery terms from the Transcription CD.

2. Transcribe the five documents from the Transcription CD following the instructions below and using the current date.

    -   Open Document 1 and use the letterhead for Simonson, Kodaly, Blum & Brathwaite. Key the document in block letter style with mixed punctuation.

    -   Open Document 2 and use the letterhead for Simonson, Kodaly, Blum & Brathwaite. Key the variable information on the underlines in the document, and then remove the underlines.

    -   Open Document 3 and use the letterhead for Simonson, Kodaly, Blum & Brathwaite. Key the variable information on the underlines in the document, and then remove the underlines.

    -   Open Document 4 and use the Last Will and Testament form. Key the variable information on the underlines in the document, and then remove the underlines.

    -   Open Document 5 and use the Durable Power of Attorney form. Key the variable information on the underlines in the document, and then remove the underlines. Also, key the additional information to be included on the form as dictated.

3. When you have transcribed a document using the file from the Transcription CD, remember to use the *Save As* feature and a distinctive name as the file name for each document.

4. Spell-check, proofread, and submit all five documents to your instructor for approval.

CHAPTER CHECKPOINTS

Place a check mark beside the objectives you can meet after completing this chapter.

_____ I can define, spell, and use the Word Mastery terms in this chapter.

_____ I can use the commonly misused terms from the Word Usage section in this chapter.

_____ I can spell correctly the words in the Spelling section in this chapter.

_____ I can apply the rules for word division presented in the Language Skills section in this chapter and other punctuation and grammar rules presented in earlier chapters.

_____ I can transcribe form letters and proofread carefully.

_____ I can transcribe legal documents, including a Last Will and Testament and a Power of Attorney, and proofread carefully.

Evaluation Form

Access the Evaluation Form from your Transcription CD. Complete it and submit it with your work. You may choose to either print the form and complete it or complete the form electronically.

©auremar/Shutterstock.com

Chapter 17

CONSULTATION LETTER, MEDICAL MEMORANDUM, MAMMOGRAM REPORT, AND HISTORY AND PHYSICAL REPORT

The medical field provides one of the most exciting opportunities for employment. Careers await trained personnel in private doctors' offices, hospitals, clinics, insurance companies, nursing homes, and outpatient facilities. In all areas of the United States, the medical field is expanding. As people's life spans increase, the need for medical services will continue to grow. The services of nurses and doctors are in high demand.

Medical transcriptionists and medical office personnel occupy important positions in all types of medical facilities. Because some medical terms and names of medicines are similar, medical transcriptionists must be extremely accurate in their work. Courses in medical terminology, anatomy, and biology are essential for anyone who wants to consider medical transcription as a career.

Word Mastery Preview

Directions: Review the list of Word Mastery terms that will be used in the documents you will be transcribing. Learn the definition for each word and how to spell it correctly.

cardiovascular	*Definition:*	involving the heart and the blood vessels
	Example:	Regular exercise contributes to the health of the cardiovascular system.
arteriogram	*Definition:*	an x-ray of an artery
	Example:	An arteriogram is performed when a cardiologist suspects a heart blockage.
infarction	*Definition:*	the formation of a portion of dying or dead tissue
	Example:	The formation of a blood clot is a common cause of infarction.
mammogram	*Definition:*	an x-ray of the breast
	Example:	A regular mammogram is recommended for women as an early detection of breast cancer.
calcifications	*Definition:*	deposits of calcium salts in body tissue
	Example:	Calcifications in soft tissue are abnormal.
intraductal	*Definition:*	within a duct
	Example:	The dye was injected into the body by an intraductal method.
carcinoma	*Definition:*	a malignant new growth made up of cells tending to spread to surrounding tissues; a form of cancer
	Example:	Carcinoma refers to a cancerous tumor.
biopsy	*Definition:*	removal and examination of a small amount of tissue from the body
	Example:	A biopsy is often performed when a suspicious lump is found in the breast.
benign	*Definition:*	not malignant; not cancerous
	Example:	He was relieved that the tumor was benign.

| axillary | *Definition:* | pertaining to the armpit |
| | *Example:* | The axillary area is often affected as the result of a mastectomy. |

| asymmetrical | *Definition:* | dissimilarity in appearance of body parts that should appear as the same size and shape |
| | *Example:* | The right eye was slanted more than the left, causing an asymmetrical appearance. |

 Word Usage

Directions: Learn to spell and define these confusing words, which may occur within the documents you will be transcribing.

| assistance | (noun) help |
| assistants | (noun) helpers |

| bases | (noun) a chemical that is the opposite of acids; plural of base |
| basis | (noun) underlying condition; something that is established |

| defer | (verb) to postpone |
| differ | (verb) to vary or disagree |

| eminent | (adjective) well known |
| imminent | (adjective) threatening |

| later | (adverb) refers to time |
| latter | (adjective) second of two things named |

| menstrual | (adjective) relating to the female monthly cycle |
| minstrel | (adjective) relating to music or entertainment |

peal	(noun or verb) loud sound; to bring forth loudly
peel	(noun or verb) outer layer; to take off
pill	(noun) medication

C Spelling

Directions: Learn to spell these common words.

advantageous	irritable	schedule
athlete	medicine	scissors
criticism	minuscule	technique
desperate	professional	valuable
intimate	relevant	welcome

Tips

- Use the *Print Preview* feature of Microsoft Word to review a document prior to printing. In this layout, you can view a reduced size of your document on the computer screen. By viewing the document at one glance, you can check the format, alignment, etc.

- By using the *Print Preview* feature, you can reduce excessive printing and wastage of paper. Using less paper saves money, trees, and landfill space.

D Language Skills

Directions: Knowing various prefixes and suffixes used within the medical fields will help you become more familiar with the meanings of medical terms. In the Language Skills section of this chapter and Chapters 18 through 20, you will be introduced to various prefixes and suffixes. Some of these prefixes and suffixes are used in the Word Mastery terms you are studying within the chapter. Learn each prefix or suffix and its meaning.

Prefix or Suffix	Meaning
ambi-	on both sides
anti-	against
arterio-	artery
auto-	self
bi-	two
carcino-	carcinoma
cardio-	heart
-gram	record
intra-	within
mammo-	breast

ENGLISH SKILLS EXERCISES

A Word Mastery

Directions: Apply what you learned in the English Skills Review. Choose the correct word in the following sentences from those found in the Word Mastery Preview.

1. Sylvia always has her _____ done on a yearly basis as a preventative measure against breast cancer.

2. When the doctors examined the x-rays more closely, they decided that the areas of concern were merely _____ in the body tissue.

3. After the mammogram was performed, the doctors could tell more from the _____ taken from her left breast.

4. Ralph hoped his tumor was _____ and not malignant.

5. Sometimes tissue from the _____ area must be removed if breast cancer has been found.

6. The _____ appearance of his ears made him look quite unusual.

7. Since he did not exercise and watch what he ate, it is no surprise that he had _____ disease at an early age.

8. _____ is a form of cancer.

9. If your physician suspects some heart blockage, he may perform a(n) _____.

10. A(n) _____ can occur if you have a blood clot.

B Word Usage

Directions: Choose the correct word in each of the following sentences.

1. Many women experience pain during their monthly (menstrual, minstrel) cycle.

2. Why don't you take the pain (peal, peel, pill) your doctor prescribed instead of trying to endure it?

3. Since the physician hired two new (assistance, assistants), I am not placed on hold as often when I call.

4. Acids neutralize (bases, basis) in a chemical reaction.

5. The nurse practitioner will (defer, differ) her comments until she has consulted the primary care physician.

6. Watching the clouds roll over the hill, the bride knew that rain was (eminent, imminent) and that her outdoor wedding would have to be moved to an indoor venue.

7. Drama and comedy are two types of entertainment; the (later, latter) makes you laugh.

8. Although we (defer, differ) in our opinion about the medical facility's new color scheme, we both agree that it is bright and cheery.

9. The (eminent, imminent) surgeon treated each of her patients with care and respect.

10. If you need my (assistance, assistants) in learning the medical codes, let me know.

C Spelling

Directions: Choose the correct spelling in each of the following sentences.

1. Because she is an (athelete, athlete), she knows how (valuable, valueable) proper diet and exercise are for good health.

2. Shenika didn't like to take the (medecine, medicine) her physician prescribed because she felt it made her (irritible, irritable).

3. Some female patients don't feel comfortable discussing (intamate, intimate) medical concerns with a male medical (professional, proffessional).

4. The (scissers, scissors) were so (miniscule, minuscule) that she thought they were made for children.

5. It would be (advantagous, advantageous) for you to lose eight pounds before your office visit next month.

6. A good medical office professional will (welcome, wellcome) patients with a smile and give them her or his undivided attention.

Spelling (*continued*)

7. Which (technigue, technique) will you use to convince your child to go to the pediatrician's office?

8. Roger was (desperate, disperate) to find a way to stop smoking.

9. I don't think your suggestion is (relavant, relevant) to this situation.

10. (Criticisim, Criticism) is not the best way to encourage someone to exercise.

D Language Skills

Directions: Use proofreaders' marks to make corrections in the following sentences. Write "Correct" by the sentence if no corrections are needed. Some of these sentences include a review of language skills presented in previous chapters. You may want to refer to the reference manual in the back of this text-workbook for a review before completing these examples.

1. Our medical office will now be located at 23 East 5th Avenue.

2. We found $.50 under the sofa when we were cleaning the physician's office.

3. The medical secretary informed the physician he had eleven more patients in the waiting room to see him.

4. After studying for the test, the student felt she still did not know fifty percent of the medical prefixes and suffixes.

5. Manuel Martinez had an appointment on the 5 of May to see his physician.

6. Your doctor's appointment was scheduled for June 5.

7. There is an 80% chance he will recover from the accident.

8. Please visit our new location at 1 West 10th Avenue.

9. Your bill for the office visit today will be $95.00.

10. Of the 10 nurses hired last year, 2 decided to resign.

Fill in the medical prefixes or suffixes for the meanings listed below:

record   _____

breast   _____

heart   _____

artery   _____

within   _____

E Composition

1. Compose and key a paragraph applying the word mastery, word usage, spelling, and language skills you have studied.

2. Compose and key a second paragraph that explains why seeing a physician is important to good health.

3. Compose and key a third paragraph that explains how someone can benefit from knowing medical prefixes and suffixes. Submit all three paragraphs to your instructor.

F Research

1. Conduct research using the Internet, newspaper, and library or talk with individuals who are actually employed in the medical field to obtain information about the topics listed below. When searching online, go to the U.S. Bureau of Labor Statistics website at **www.bls.gov** and click on the **Publications** tab. Then click on the *Occupational Outlook Handbook* and **Index** links. Click on the first letter of the name of the field. (Example: Click on the letter *M* and scroll down the screen to find information on *medical*.) You can also do an online search of the name of the field/industry followed by the words *career* or *training*. (Example: *medical career* or *medical training*)

   • What are the employment opportunities for office workers in the medical field?

   • What are the advantages and/or disadvantages of employment in this field?

   • What skills or characteristics are necessary for someone who wants to work in this field?

   • What are the job titles or positions in this field?

   • What are the salary ranges for positions in this field?

   • What additional information did you learn during this research?

2. Compose and key paragraphs that address the questions above. Add a meaningful title. Include your name and the date. Proofread, edit, and revise the paragraphs to correct all grammar and spelling errors. Print the document. Proofread it again and make any final changes before submitting it to your instructor.

TRANSCRIPTION PREVIEW

In this chapter you will key five documents, including a Mammogram Report and a History and Physical Report. Become familiar with these reports by reviewing the examples that follow. Because you are just beginning to transcribe medical documents and the terminology is challenging, you will be required to key information into a report that has already been partially completed for you.

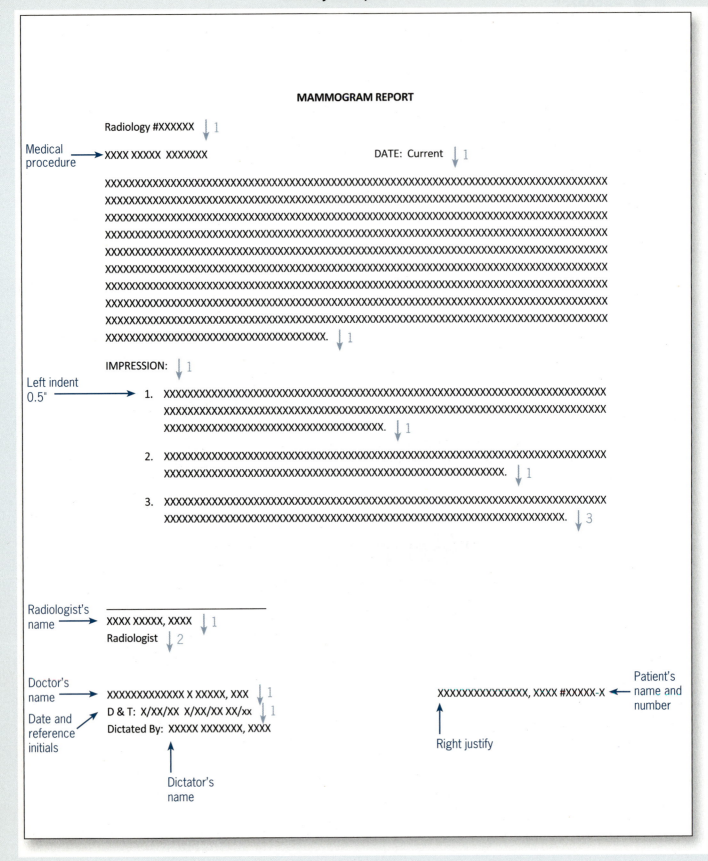

MAMMOGRAM REPORT

Radiology #XXXXXX ↓1

Medical procedure → XXXX XXXXX XXXXXX   DATE: Current ↓1

XXXXXXXXXXXXXXXXXXXXXXXXXXXXXXXXXXXXXXXXXXXXXXXXXXXXXXXXXXXXXXXXX
XXXXXXXXXXXXXXXXXXXXXXXXXXXXXXXXXXXXXXXXXXXXXXXXXXXXXXXXXXXXXXXXX
XXXXXXXXXXXXXXXXXXXXXXXXXXXXXXXXXXXXXXXXXXXXXXXXXXXXXXXXXXXXXXXXX
XXXXXXXXXXXXXXXXXXXXXXXXXXXXXXXXXXXXXXXXXXXXXXXXXXXXXXXXXXXXXXXXX
XXXXXXXXXXXXXXXXXXXXXXXXXXXXXXXXXXXXXXXXXXXXXXXXXXXXXXXXXXXXXXXXX
XXXXXXXXXXXXXXXXXXXXXXXXXXXXXXXXXXXXXXXXXXXXXXXXXXXXXXXXXXXXXXXXX
XXXXXXXXXXXXXXXXXXXXXXXXXXXXXXXXXXXXXXXXXXXXXXXXXXXXXXXXXXXXXXXXX
XXXXXXXXXXXXXXXXXXXXXXXXXXXXXXXXXXXXXXXXXXXXXXXXXXXXXXXXXXXXXXXXX
XXXXXXXXXXXXXXXXXXXXXXXXXXXXXXXXXXXXXXXXXXXXXXXXXXXXXXXXXXXXXXXXX
XXXXXXXXXXXXXXXXXXXXXXXXXXXXXXXXXX. ↓1

IMPRESSION: ↓1

Left indent 0.5" →
1. XXXXXXXXXXXXXXXXXXXXXXXXXXXXXXXXXXXXXXXXXXXXXXXXXXXXXXXXXXXX
   XXXXXXXXXXXXXXXXXXXXXXXXXXXXXXXXXXXXXXXXXXXXXXXXXXXXXXXXXXXX
   XXXXXXXXXXXXXXXXXXXXXXXXXXXXXXX. ↓1

2. XXXXXXXXXXXXXXXXXXXXXXXXXXXXXXXXXXXXXXXXXXXXXXXXXXXXXXXXXXXX
   XXXXXXXXXXXXXXXXXXXXXXXXXXXXXXXXXXXXXXXXXX. ↓1

3. XXXXXXXXXXXXXXXXXXXXXXXXXXXXXXXXXXXXXXXXXXXXXXXXXXXXXXXXXXXX
   XXXXXXXXXXXXXXXXXXXXXXXXXXXXXXXXXXXXXXXXXXXXXXX. ↓3

Radiologist's name →
———————————————
XXXX XXXXX, XXXX ↓1
Radiologist ↓2

Doctor's name → XXXXXXXXXXXXX X XXXXX, XXX ↓1   XXXXXXXXXXXXXXX, XXXX #XXXXX-X ← Patient's name and number
Date and reference initials → D & T: X/XX/XX X/XX/XX XX/xx ↓1
Dictated By: XXXXX XXXXXXX, XXXX

Dictator's name ↑   ↑ Right justify

GASTROENTEROLOGY ASSOCIATES, P.A.
Suite 50, Building 200
80 Pelham Road
Greer, SC 29650
Phone (864) 555-7229 FAX (864) 555-8410

Patient Name: _____

Date: _____

Physician: _____

CHIEF COMPLAINT: _____

HISTORY OF PRESENT ILLNESS: _____

_____

_____

_____

_____

_____

_____

_____

_____

PAST MEDICAL HISTORY: GERD. Hemorrhoids with rare rectal bleeding. Hypertension. Hyperlipidemia. Arthritis. Colonoscopy February of this year with internal hemorrhoids. EGD July two years ago with nasopharyngeal reflex and erosive gastritis.

ALLERGIES: _____

MEDICATIONS: Nexium 40 mg, 1 p.o. b.i.d., Toprol 100 mg, 1 p.o. daily, Hyzaar, 50-12.5 mg, 1 p.o. daily, Lipitor 10 mg, 1 p.o. daily, Fibercon 625 mg, 1 p.p. daily, Glucosamine Chondrotin Complex 1 p.o. b.i.d.. Obtained medication information verbally from the patient.

PAST SURGICAL HISTORY: _____

_____

_____

SOCIAL HISTORY: _____

_____

_____

_____

FAMILY HISTORY: _____

_____

_____

_____

(Continued)

NOTE: The History and Physical Report is preprinted as shown above. Key the information dictated in the underlined spaces and then remove the underlines.

HISTORY AND PHYSICAL EXAMINATION   2
Patient Name: _____

PHYSICAL EXAMINATION:

GENERAL: _____

VITAL SIGNS: VS-Pulse: 72, right radial, regular; VS-Blood Pressure: 120/80, right arm, sitting; VS-Respiration: 18; VS-Height: 5 ft. 4 in; VS-Weight: 180 lbs; BMI: 37.59.

SKIN: Extremities and face reveal no rashes. No palmar erythema.

HEENT: Sclerae anicteric. No oral ulcerations or abnormal pigment of the lips. Pupils equal and extraocular muscles intact. Neck is supple and symmetric.

CARDIOVASCULAR: Regular rate and rhythm. No murmurs, gallops, or rubs.

ABDOMEN: Soft, nondistended, and nontender. Normal active bowel sounds. No enlargement of the liver or spleen. No masses palpable.

RECTAL: Deferred.

MUSCULOSKELETAL: Gait appears steady. No pitting edema of the lower legs. Extremities have good range of motion.

NEUROLOGICAL: Gross memory appears intact. Patient is alert and oriented times 3.

PSYCHIATRIC: Mood appears appropriate with judgment intact.

LABORATORY DATA:_____

ASSESSMENT: _____
_____
_____

PLAN: _____
_____

                                          _____
                                          _____

XX:xx

D: _____

T: _____

Copies to: _____

1. Transcribe the Word Mastery terms from the Transcription CD.

2. Transcribe the five documents from the Transcription CD following the instructions below and using the current date unless another date is given.

   - Open Document 1 and use the letterhead for Vanessa T. Melvin, M.D. Key the document in block letter style with mixed punctuation.

   - Open Document 2 and use the letterhead for Peachtree Professional Park. Key the document in memorandum format.

   - Open Document 3 and use the Mammogram Report. Key the information in the appropriate spaces on the form.

   - Open Document 4 and use the Mammogram Report. Key the information in the appropriate spaces on the form.

   - Open Document 5 and use the History and Physical form. Key the information on the underlines in the document, and then remove the underlines.

3. When you have transcribed a document using the file from the Transcription CD, remember to use the *Save As* feature and a distinctive file name.

4. Spell-check, proofread, and submit all five documents to your instructor.

CHAPTER CHECKPOINTS

Place a check mark beside the objectives you can meet after completing this chapter.

_____ I can define, spell, and use the Word Mastery terms in this chapter.

_____ I can use the commonly misused terms from the Word Usage section in this chapter.

_____ I can spell correctly the words in the Spelling section in this chapter.

_____ I can apply the medical prefixes and suffixes in this chapter.

_____ I can apply the rules from the Language Skills sections in earlier chapters.

_____ I can transcribe medical letters, memorandums, and reports, including a Mammogram Report and a History and Physical Report, and proofread carefully.

✳ Evaluation Form

Access the Evaluation Form from your Transcription CD. Complete it and submit it with your work. You may choose to either print the form and complete it or complete the form electronically.

©Orange Line Media/Shutterstock.com

LEARNING OBJECTIVES

After completing all the learning activities in this chapter, you will be able to:

- Define, spell, and use the Word Mastery terms.

- Use commonly misused words appropriately.

- Use correct spelling for commonly misspelled words.

- Apply medical prefixes and suffixes presented in this chapter.

- Apply the language skills rules presented in earlier chapters.

- Apply proofreading and transcription skills.

- Transcribe radiology reports and letters.

Chapter 18

RADIOLOGY REPORT, RELOCATION ANNOUNCEMENT, AND LIFESAVING SCREENING LETTER

Patients today may choose to have routine x-rays done at an outpatient radiology facility as a less costly alternative to hospital admission and testing. Radiology offices provide another career opportunity for medical transcriptionists. Results from procedures involving anteroposterior (AP) x-ray, nuclear medicine, low-dose mammography, ultrasound, computed tomography (CT), and magnetic resonance imaging (MRI) must be transcribed into a variety of reports.

A Word Mastery Preview

Directions: Review the list of Word Mastery terms that will be used in the documents you will be transcribing. Learn the definition for each word and how to spell it correctly.

demineralization	*Definition:*	excessive elimination of mineral or organic salts from the tissues of the body
	Example:	Digesting one thousand milligrams of calcium per day can help prevent demineralization of the bones.
degenerative	*Definition:*	deteriorating
	Example:	Degenerative arthritis can be very painful.
arthritic	*Definition:*	pertaining to the inflammation of a joint
	Example:	The Arthritis Foundation supports research for arthritis to help sufferers of arthritic pain lead productive lives.
spurring	*Definition:*	the projection of a growth that extends from the bone
	Example:	Spinal arthritic spurring can cause a patient great discomfort.
spondylolisthesis	*Definition:*	forward displacement of a vertebra over a lower portion of the spine due to an inborn defect or fracture
	Example:	For temporary relief of spondylolisthesis, the patient saw the chiropractor for spinal manipulation.
apophyseal	*Definition:*	pertaining to any outgrowth or swelling, especially a bony outgrowth that has never been entirely separated from the bone of which it forms a part
	Example:	The apophyseal joints were best demonstrated on the lumbar views.
levoscoliosis	*Definition:*	a left-sided abnormal curving of the spinal column
	Example:	Levoscoliosis can cause neck and back pain.

acute	*Definition:*	sudden; sharp; severe
	Example:	An acute illness is serious but only lasts for a short period of time.

aorta	*Definition:*	the largest artery in the body, arising from the left ventricle of the heart; the main trunk from which the systemic arterial system proceeds.
	Example:	The aorta is the largest artery in the body.

magnetic resonance imaging (MRI)	*Definition:*	an imaging technique used to diagnose cancer and other tumors and masses of the soft tissues
	Example:	A patient must lie motionless in the center of a tube during the magnetic resonance imaging process.

B Word Usage

Directions: Learn to spell and define these confusing words, which may occur within the documents you will be transcribing.

core	(noun) the center or vital part
corps	(noun) an organized group of persons
corpse	(noun) a dead body

detract	(verb) to take away from
distract	(verb) to divert the attention of

defuse	(verb) to resolve
diffuse	(verb) to disperse

famous	(adjective) well known for something positive
infamous	(adjective) well known for something negative

lead	(verb or noun) to guide or direct; a heavy metal
led	(verb) past tense of the verb *lead*

patience	(noun) calm endurance
patients	(noun) persons receiving medical treatment

perquisite	(noun) a privilege or benefit
prerequisite	(noun) a preliminary requirement

Spelling

Directions: Learn to spell these common words.

aggression	inoculate	permanent
conscious	laboratory	strength
disappoint	mysterious	transferring
generally	operate	verify
guidance	opportunity	vicious

 Language Skills

Directions: Knowing various prefixes and suffixes used within the medical fields will help you become more familiar with the meanings of medical terms. Some of these prefixes and suffixes are used in the Word Mastery terms you are studying within the chapter. Learn each prefix or suffix and its meaning.

Prefix or Suffix	Meaning
-cyte	cell
de-	lack of
di-	two, twice
-ectomy	removal
hemi-	half
hemato-	blood
inter-	between
macro-	large
micro-	small
neo-	new

Proofreading Tips

- Take advantage of the spelling and grammar check tool in your word processing program. It will flag misspelled words and grammatical errors as well as provide suggestions on how to correct them.

- Although some errors will be detected, do not rely totally on the spelling and grammar check tool to find all of the errors. For example, find the five errors that the spelling and grammar check tool did not find in the sentence below.

  When you leaf the doctors office be sure to take your peals when you get to you're home.

  The correct version of the sentence is as follows. (The undetected errors are shown in bold.)

  *When you **leave** the **doctor's** office**,** be sure to take your **pills** when you get to **your** home.*

ENGLISH SKILLS EXERCISES

 Word Mastery

Directions: Apply what you learned in the English Skills Review. Choose the correct word in the following sentences from those found in the Word Mastery Preview.

1. Her doctor thought the pain was from _____ arthritis.

2. Those who suffer from _____ can often find relief from pain by visiting a chiropractor for adjustment of the spine.

3. Many children are checked for _____ when they visit their pediatricians for a yearly physical.

4. Her _____ headache even caused her to have vision problems.

5. Although she was scared to have the _____ performed, she discovered there was no pain involved.

6. _____ pain occurs in many senior adults as the body ages.

7. Arthritic _____ causes severe pain.

8. The doctor prescribed calcium to his patient to help prevent _____ of her bones.

9. The _____ is an artery in the heart.

10. When the doctor looked at the x-rays, he could see the _____ joints.

B Word Usage

Directions: Choose the correct word in each of the following sentences.

1. Bonnie and Clyde were (famous, infamous) for robbing banks.

2. Will you (lead, led) the class into the auditorium for graduation?

3. Don't you think your casual attire will (detract, distract) your audience when you make your presentation?

4. Wiley and Jackie have more (patience, patients) than they did when they were both working outside the home and caring for five small children.

5. When will they move the (core, corps, corpse) from the hospital?

6. Sean did not realize he had not taken the last (perquisite, prerequisite) for the course in medical transcription.

7. The scent of gardenias will (diffuse, defuse) throughout the room.

8. Please put the apple (core, corps, corpse) in the garbage when you finish eating your snack.

9. There were only five (patience, patients) in the waiting room when I arrived for my appointment with the radiologist.

10. My gynecologist is (famous, infamous) for giving his time and services to the local free medical clinic.

C Spelling

Directions: Choose the correct spelling in each of the following sentences.

1. The nurse will (inoculate, innoculate) my child while I hold him still with all the (strenght, strength) I have.

2. The doctor withheld giving his diagnosis until he had received the report from the (labatory, laboratory).

3. If you don't want to (disappoint, dissapoint) your parents, why don't you seek their (guidance, guideance) before making poor choices in life?

4. After the (vicious, vicous) dog attack, the child was not (conscious, conseous).

5. The hospital was (transfering, transferring) the patient to another facility where a physician agreed to (operate, opperate) on the individual.

6. Will you have an (opportunity, oppurtunity) to (verefy, verify) the report before making a final decision?

7. Don't let your (agression, aggression) show.

8. (Generally, Generaly), we prefer to see our primary care physician instead of the nurse practitioner.

9. We hope that the scars will not be (permanent, perminent).

10. His disappearance was so (mysterious, mystereous) to everyone.

D Language Skills

Directions: Use proofreaders' marks to make corrections in the following sentences. Write "Correct" by the sentence if no corrections are needed. Some of these sentences include a review of language skills presented in previous chapters. You may want to refer to the reference manual in the back of this text-workbook for a review before completing these examples.

1. The interns will need to attend the orientation meeting at 3 o'clock.

2. Check the patient's blood pressure, temperature, and other vital signs—these are the procedures she is to follow.

3. If and only if you must leave the class, be sure you ask someone to take notes for you.

4. This is an emergency.

5. The following students will be graduating from the program Tomas Medina, Margarita Flores, and Oki Beppu.

6. Anatomy pathology and pharmacology these courses need to be taken before you proceed with the medical transcription course.

7. I must stress that you follow the directions carefully very carefully when taking this medication.

8. The surgery will begin at four p.m. tomorrow afternoon.

9. The surgical room is on fire.

10. The following reports were typed by the medical transcriptionist within the past hour radiology report, history and physical report, and pathology report.

Language Skills (*continued*)

Fill in the prefixes or suffixes for the meanings listed below:

cell _____

lack of _____

blood _____

between _____

new _____

E Composition

1. Compose and key a paragraph applying the word mastery, word usage, spelling, and language skills you have studied.

2. Compose and key a second paragraph that describes the type of training a radiologist may require.

3. Compose and key a third paragraph that compares CT and PET scans. Submit all three paragraphs to your instructor.

F Research

1. Locate five recent articles from newspapers, magazines, the library, or the Internet that relate to medical ethics, medical cases, medical documents, medical terminology, or the medical profession.

2. List the source and date of each article and summarize it in paragraph format. Include your name and the date. Proofread, edit, and revise the paragraphs to correct all grammar and spelling errors. Print the documents. Proofread them again and make any final changes before submitting them to your instructor.

TRANSCRIPTION PREVIEW

In this chapter you will key five documents, including radiology reports. The format of radiology reports can vary depending on the medical facility's preference and the type of procedure performed. Review the examples that follow to become familiar with the various radiology report formats that will be used in this chapter. You will key information into the preprinted forms.

Great Lakes Associates in Radiology and Imaging
777 St. Clair Avenue
Cleveland, OH 44114-3144
Phone: (216) 555-6789
Fax: (216) 555-6799

Patient's Name	Age		Address	X-Ray No.
XXXXXXXX	(X/XX/--) XX		XXXXXXXX	XXX
Guarantor	Telephone		XXXXXXXXXXXXX	Date
XXXXX	(XXX) XXX-XXXX			X/X/--
S.S. No.	Insurance Information			Referring Physician
XXXXXXXXX	XXXXXXXXXXXXXXXX			XXXXXXX
Previous Exam				Exam Requested
XX				XXXXXXX
History	Place of Employment			XX
XX	XX			

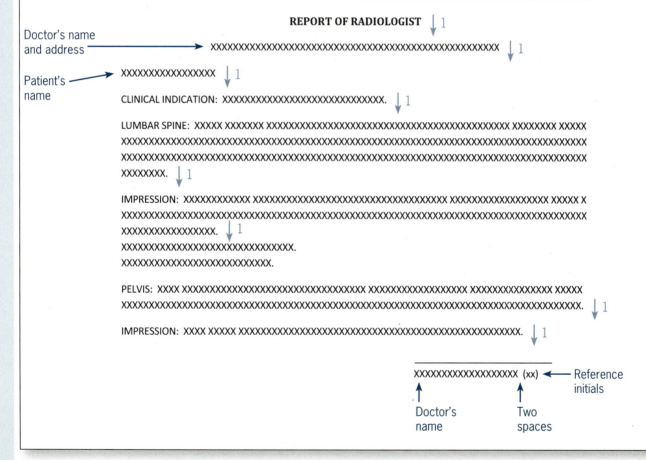

REPORT OF RADIOLOGIST ↓1

Doctor's name and address → XXXXXXXXXXXXXXXXXXXXXXXXXXXXXXXXXXXXXXXXXXXXXXXXXX ↓1

Patient's name → XXXXXXXXXXXXXXXX ↓1

CLINICAL INDICATION: XXXXXXXXXXXXXXXXXXXXXXXXXXXXXXX. ↓1

LUMBAR SPINE: XXXXX XXXXXXX XXXXXXXXXXXXXXXXXXXXXXXXXXXXXXXXXXXXXXXX XXXXXXXX XXXXX
XXXXXXXXXXXXXXXXXXXXXXXXXXXXXXXXXXXXXXXXXXXXXXXXXXXXXXXXXXXXXXXXXXXXXXXXXXXX
XXXXXXXXXXXXXXXXXXXXXXXXXXXXXXXXXXXXXXXXXXXXXXXXXXXXXXXXXXXXXXXXXXXXXXXXXXXX
XXXXXXXX. ↓1

IMPRESSION: XXXXXXXXXXX XXXXXXXXXXXXXXXXXXXXXXXXXXXXXXXXX XXXXXXXXXXXXXXXXX XXXXX X
XXXXXXXXXXXXXXXXXXXXXXXXXXXXXXXXXXXXXXXXXXXXXXXXXXXXXXXXXXXXXXXXXXXXXXXXXXXX
XXXXXXXXXXXXXXXX. ↓1
XXXXXXXXXXXXXXXXXXXXXXXXXXXXXXX.
XXXXXXXXXXXXXXXXXXXXXXXXXXXXX.

PELVIS: XXXX XXXXXXXXXXXXXXXXXXXXXXXXXXXX XXXXXXXXXXXXXX XXXXXXXXXXXXXX XXXXX
XXXXXXXXXXXXXXXXXXXXXXXXXXXXXXXXXXXXXXXXXXXXXXXXXXXXXXXXXXXXXXXXXXX. ↓1

IMPRESSION: XXXX XXXXX XXXXXXXXXXXXXXXXXXXXXXXXXXXXXXXXXXXXXXXXXXXXXX. ↓1

_____

XXXXXXXXXXXXXXXXXX (xx) ← Reference initials

↑ Doctor's name   ↑ Two spaces

NOTE: The top portion and the headings in Radiology Report (1) are preprinted as shown above. Key the information dictated in the appropriate spaces on the form.

RADIOLOGY ASSOCIATES
Suite 200, Building A
1200 Mountain Road
Spokane, WA 99210

Patient's Name: XXXXXXXXXXXXX

Patient's Social Security Number: XXX-XX-XXX

Procedure Ordered: XXXXXXXXXXXXXXXXXXXXXXXXXXXXXXXXX

Exam Date: XXXXXXXXX, XX, XXXX

Physician: XXXXXXXXXX, XXXXXXX

Imaging Location: XXXXXXXXXXXXXXXXXXXXXXXXXXXX

Case XXX XXXXXXXXXXXXXXXXXXXXXXXXXXXXXXXXXXXXXXXX

Reason for Study: XXXXXXXXXXXXXXXXX

Clinical History: XXXXXXXXXXXXXXXXXXXXXXXXXXXXXXXX

Report Status: XXXXXXXXX

Date Reported: XXXXXXXXX, XX, XXXX

Date Verified: XXXXXXXXX, XX, XXXX

Verifier: XXXXXXXXX XXXXXXXXX

Report: XXXXXXXXXXXXXXXXXXXXXXXXXXXXXXXXXXXXXXXXXXXXXXXXXXXXXXXXXXXXXXXXXXXXXXXXXXX
XXXXXXXXXXXXXXXXXXXXXXXXXXXXXXXXXXXXXXXXXXXXXXXXXXXXXXXXXXXXXXXXXXXXXXXXXXXXXXXXXXX
XXXXXXXXXXXXXXXXXXXXXXXXXXXXXXXXXXXXXXXXXXXXXXXXXXXXXXXXXXXXXXXXXXXXXXXXXXXXXXXXXXX
XXXXXXXXXXXXXXXXXXXXXXXXXXXXXXXXXXXXXXXXXXXXXXXXXXX

Impression: XXXXXXXXXXXXXXXXXXXXXXXXXXX

Primary Interpreting Staff: XXXXXXXXX XXXXXXXXXX XXXXXXXXXXX

NOTE: **Radiology Report (2) is preprinted with the headings as shown above. Key the information dictated next to the appropriate headings.**

GREENVILLE RADIOLOGY
1210 W. Farris Road
Greenville, NC 27833
Phone: 252.555.4567

Referring Physician: Randy Vaughan, M.D.

In reference to your recent referral of patient:

Mary Elizabeth Harris
12 South Main Street
Greenville, NC 27833

UNLISTED CT OR CARDIAC SCORING

CT CORONARY ARTERY CALCIFICATION SCORING

HISTORY: 57-year-old female with family history of cardiac disease.

TECHNIQUE: 2.5 mm ECG gated helical subsecond images were acquired with automated motion reduction selection and manual identification of calcification along the coronary arteries. Agatston scoring system was utilized with a 130 Hounsfield unit threshold.

FINDINGS: The patient's total coronary artery calcification score is 0 placing the patient in the $0 - 10^{th}$ percentile for age and gender matched controls. This means that 90 percent of females in the 56-60 year old age range would have a higher coronary artery calcification score.

Evaluation of the immediate juxtacardiac lung parenchyma and mediastinum reveals evidence for remote healed granulomatous disease. There are subcentimeter calcified granulomas present in the medial right lung base with calcified right hilar and subcarinal subcentimeter lymph nodes present as well as an approximate 4 mm calcified granuloma in the central left lung base.

I see no evidence for noncalcified pulmonary nodule or juxtacardiac mediastinal adenopathy. A small hiatal hernia is noted.

CONCLUSIONS: ↓1

1. XXXXXXXXXXXXXXXXXXXXXXXXXXXXXXXXXXXXXXXXXXXXXXXXXXXXXXXXXXXXXXXXXXXXXXXXXXXX
XXXXXXXXXXXXXXXXXXXXXXXXXXXXXXXXXXXXXXXXXXXXXXXXXXXXXXXXXXX. ↓1

2. XXXXXXXXXXXXXXXXXXXXXXXXXXXXXXXXXXXXXXXXXXXXXXXXXXXXXXXXXXXXXXXXXXXXXXXXXXXX
XXXXXXXXXXXXXXXXXXXXXXXXXXXX. ↓1

3. XXXXXXXXXXXXXXXXXXXXXXXXXXXXXXXXXXXXXXXXXXXXXXXXXXXXXXXXXXXXXXXXX. ↓2

Doctor's name ——► XXXXXXXXX XXXXXXXXXXXXXX

NOTE: The top portion of Radiology Report (3) is preprinted as shown above. Key the information dictated in the *Conclusions* section.

TRANSCRIPTION EXERCISES

1. Transcribe the Word Mastery terms from the Transcription CD.

2. Transcribe the five documents from the Transcription CD following the instructions below and using the current date unless another date is given.

   - Open Document 1 and use the radiologist's report for Great Lakes Associates in Radiology and Imaging. Key the information in the appropriate spaces on the form.

   - Open Document 2 and use the letterhead for Great Lakes Associates in Radiology and Imaging. Key the document in modified block style with mixed punctuation.

   - Open Document 3 and use the radiologist's report for Radiology Associates. Key the information in the appropriate spaces on the form.

   - Open Document 4 and use the radiologist's report for Greenville Radiology. Key the information in the appropriate spaces on the form.

   - Open Document 5 and use the letterhead for Florida Lifesaving Screening. Key the document in block letter style with mixed punctuation.

3. When you have transcribed a document using the file from the Transcription CD, remember to use the **Save As** feature and a distinctive name as the file name for each document.

4. Spell-check, proofread, and submit all five documents to your instructor for approval.

CHAPTER CHECKPOINTS

Place a check mark beside the objectives
you can meet after completing this chapter.

_____ I can define, spell, and use the Word Mastery terms in this chapter.

_____ I can use the commonly misused terms from the Word Usage section in this chapter.

_____ I can spell correctly the words in the Spelling section in this chapter.

_____ I can apply the medical prefixes and suffixes in this chapter.

_____ I can apply the rules from the Language Skills sections in earlier chapters.

_____ I can transcribe radiology reports and letters and proofread carefully.

Evaluation Form

Access the Evaluation Form from your Transcription CD. Complete it and
submit it with your work. You may choose to either print the form and
complete it or complete the form electronically.

© Lisa F. Young/Shutterstock.com

Chapter 19

MEDICAL TRANSCRIPTIONIST JOB DESCRIPTION, OPERATIVE REPORT, DENTAL REPORT, DENTAL LETTER, AND ENDODONTIST LETTER

Typically, family dentistry has focused on the care and treatment of the gums and teeth. Like other fields of medicine, dentists today can also specialize in various areas of dentistry. Specialists include the endodonist, who does root canal work; the oral surgeon, who specializes in jaw surgery and extractions; the orthodontist, who is skilled in straightening teeth; the pedodontist, who specializes in dental care for children; the periodontist, who treats gum disease; and the prosthodontist, who makes dentures and artificial teeth.

Word Mastery Preview

Directions: Review the list of Word Mastery terms that will be used in the documents you will be transcribing. Learn the definition for each word and how to spell it correctly.

periodontal	*Definition:*	the area around a tooth
	Example:	Periodontal comes from peri meaning surrounding, odonto meaning teeth, and al meaning pertaining to.
endotracheal	*Definition:*	within the trachea, the main trunk by which air passes to and from the lungs
	Example:	An endotracheal tube may be placed into the trachea through the mouth to establish an airway.
subgingival	*Definition:*	beneath the gingiva, the teeth-bearing portion of the gum
	Example:	Proper brushing, flossing, and use of a dental irrigating device will help to avoid subgingival dental problems.
calculus	*Definition:*	an abnormal hardening composed of mineral salts occurring within the body; stones
	Example:	To ensure good dental health, calculus must periodically be cleaned from teeth.
supragingival	*Definition:*	above the gingiva, the teeth-bearing portion of the gum
	Example:	Supragingival and subgingival disease is treated by a periodontist.
Titan scaler	*Definition:*	a dental instrument used to remove calculus from teeth
	Example:	A Titan scaler was used by the hygienist to scrape calculus from the patient's teeth.
prophylaxis	*Definition:*	prevention of disease; preventative treatment
	Example:	Dental prophylaxis is the description of the procedure used to clean patients' teeth.
sulci	*Definition:*	the plural of sulcus; grooves or furrows
	Example:	The spaces between the surface of teeth and the linings on the free surface of the gingiva are referred to as gingival sulci.

lactated Ringers	*Definition:*	a blood serum substitute used to replace blood lost in emergencies
	Example:	Lactated Ringers is a solution for blood or serum.

Novocaln	*Definition:*	an anesthetic
	Example:	The dentist gave the patient an injection of Novocain prior to extracting the tooth.

debris	*Definition:*	the remains of anything broken down or destroyed; fragments
	Example:	The patient rinsed her mouth to remove any debris after the cleaning of her teeth.

cuspids	*Definition:*	a conical-pointed tooth, especially one situated between the lateral incisor and the first premolar
	Example:	Sarah Katherine did not like having her cuspids removed.

cysts	*Definition:*	a closed sac having a distinct membrane and developing abnormally in a cavity or structure of the body.
	Example:	The dentist found several cysts within the area of the maxillary cuspids.

pericoronal	*Definition:*	around the crown of the tooth
	Example:	There were several cysts in the pericoronal area in the patient's teeth.

B Word Usage

Directions: Learn to spell and define these confusing words, which may occur within the documents you will be transcribing.

correspondence	(noun) letters
correspondents	(noun) letter writers

decent	(adjective) proper; right
descent	(noun) decline
dissent	(noun) disagreement or difference of opinion

foreword	(noun) preface or prologue
forward	(verb and adverb) send; ahead

| hear | (verb) listen or heed |
| here | (adverb) at this time |

| overdo | (verb) exceed or go too far |
| overdue | (adjective) unpaid or late |

| want | (verb) desire or need |
| won't | (verb) contraction for *will not* |

| your | (pronoun) belonging to you |
| you're | (pronoun plus verb) contraction for *you are* |

Spelling

Directions: Learn to spell these common words.

dissatisfied	jealous	reminiscent
exhilarate	particularly	ridiculous
extension	postpone	sincerely
extraction	pronunciation	vacuum
irrelevant	quarantine	weird

Language Skills

Directions: Knowing various prefixes and suffixes used within the medical fields will help you become more familiar with the meanings of medical terms. Some of these prefixes and suffixes are used in the Word Mastery terms you are studying within the chapter. Learn each prefix or suffix and its meaning.

Prefix or Suffix	Meaning
endo-	within
gingivo-	gums
-graphy	process of recording
-itis	inflammation
-logy	study of
-oma	tumor
peri-	around, surrounding
-plasty	surgical repair
sub-	under, below
supra-	above, over

Proofreading Tips

- Proper lighting is essential while proofreading.

- Reading a document aloud keeps you more focused on it as you proofread.

- Finding ways to relieve stress, such as listening to music or chewing gum, helps you relax as you proofread.

ENGLISH SKILLS EXERCISES

A Word Mastery

Directions: Apply what you learned in the English Skills Review. Choose the correct word in the following sentences from those found in the Word Mastery Preview.

1. Most people fear going to the dentist because of the _____ work that must be done.

2. Sometimes it feels very awkward having the _____ tube in your mouth as the dentist examines your teeth.

3. We should go to our dentists every six months for _____, which can prevent tooth decay.

4. When the dental hygienist cleans your teeth, she scrapes the _____ of your teeth to remove the build up of calculus.

5. Because people cannot take the pain involved with dental work, dentists use _____, which eliminates the sensation of pain.

6. When you have your teeth cleaned, the dental hygienist removes the _____ from your teeth.

7. _____ disease is found around the upper gum area.

8. _____ disease is found around the lower gum area.

9. As your hygienist cleans your teeth, she uses a(n) _____ to remove the calculus.

10. You can clean the _____ from your mouth by rinsing periodically as your teeth are cleaned.

B Word Usage

Directions: Choose the correct word in each of the following sentences.

1. Do you want (your, your're) dentist to refer you to an endodontist?

2. (Want, Won't) you please floss your teeth like I asked you?

3. If you (overdo, overdue) it before you are fully recovered from surgery, you may find yourself in a great deal of pain.

4. His (correspondence, correspondents) opened his mail and responded to each of his fan letters.

5. To earn a (decent, descent, dissent) living for your family, you need to complete your training so you can find gainful employment.

6. You need to move (forward, foreword) and not dwell on the mistakes you made in the past.

7. We often (hear, here) what we want to (hear, here).

8. Since the dental assistant was the dentist's wife, she knew how he would want to respond to every piece of (correspondence, correspondents) he received.

9. Many (overdo, overdue) bills were on Melinda's desk at home.

10. (Your, You're) going to be glad you attended the workshop yesterday.

C Spelling

Directions: Choose the correct spelling in each of the following sentences.

1. Madeline did not want to (postpone, postphone) having her braces removed (particularly, particulurly) because the prom was next week.

2. Many of her colleagues were (jealous, jelous) of her excellent (prenunciation, pronunciation) of each student's name at graduation.

3. My dentist will have to make only one tooth (extraction, extracsion) today; however, he did tell me I may face more in the near future.

4. I (sincerely, sincerly) feel so (rediculous, ridiculous) wearing the Big Pumpkin disguise when everyone else in the dental clinic so conveniently forgot it was Halloween.

5. The medical professional said he was going to add an (extension, extention) of two more days on the (quaranteen, quarantine) of the facility.

6. When I started to (vaccum, vacuum) the dental office, it made me think back to Saturday mornings (remenesent, reminiscent) of my childhood when I would help my mother clean the house.

7. If you are (disatisfied, dissatisfied) with your current dentist, ask your friends to recommend one to you.

8. Coffee will (exhilerate, exhilarate) me in the morning; however, too much caffeine close to bedtime will prevent me from falling asleep.

9. It seems so (weird, wierd) just wearing a retainer and not having all the dental work in my mouth.

10. Your question was totally (irrelevant, irrelivant) to our current discussion.

D Language Skills

Directions: Use proofreaders' marks to make corrections in the following sentences. Write "Correct" by the sentence if no corrections are needed. Some of these sentences include a review of language skills presented in previous chapters. You may want to refer to the reference manual in the back of this text-workbook for a review before completing these examples.

1. We need to attend meetings in Charlotte, North Carolina, Charleston, South Carolina, and Miami, Florida.

2. In 2009 45 dentists graduated from the dental school in our state.

3. My dentist said, "that he wanted me to floss my teeth every day."

4. She asked what I wanted to eat for dinner.

5. I will have to have another check up with my dentist in the Fall.

6. The dentist said I want to see you back for your check up in six months.

7. He had attended school in Raleigh North Carolina Tallahassee Florida and Atlanta Georgia.

8. On page 45 11 items were omitted in the report.

9. The medical secretary asked, "If I wanted to make an appointment."

10. The dental assistant said that she could not locate my files but would return my call as soon as she found them.

Fill in the prefixes or suffixes for the meanings listed below:

gums	_____
around, surrounding	_____
under, below	_____
tumor	_____
surgical repair	_____

E Composition

1. Compose and key a paragraph applying the word mastery, word usage, spelling, and language skills you have studied.

2. Compose and key a second paragraph that explains the importance of having regular dental checkups.

3. Compose and key a third paragraph that explains the difference between the terms *subgingival* and *supragingival*. Submit all three paragraphs to your instructor.

F Research

1. Locate five recent articles from newspapers, magazines, the library, or the Internet that relate to medical ethics, medical cases, medical documents, medical terminology, or the medical profession that you did not use in previous chapters.

2. List the source and date of each article and summarize it in paragraph format. Include your name and the date. Proofread, edit, and revise the paragraphs to correct all grammar and spelling errors. Print the documents. Proofread them again and make any final changes before submitting them to your instructor.

TRANSCRIPTION PREVIEW

In this chapter you will key five documents using plain paper, letterheads, and one form. The Job Description must be keyed on plain paper from the dictation given. The Operative Report is a preprinted form. You will listen to the dictation and key the information in the form. Review the examples that follow to become familiar with the Job Description and the Operative Report.

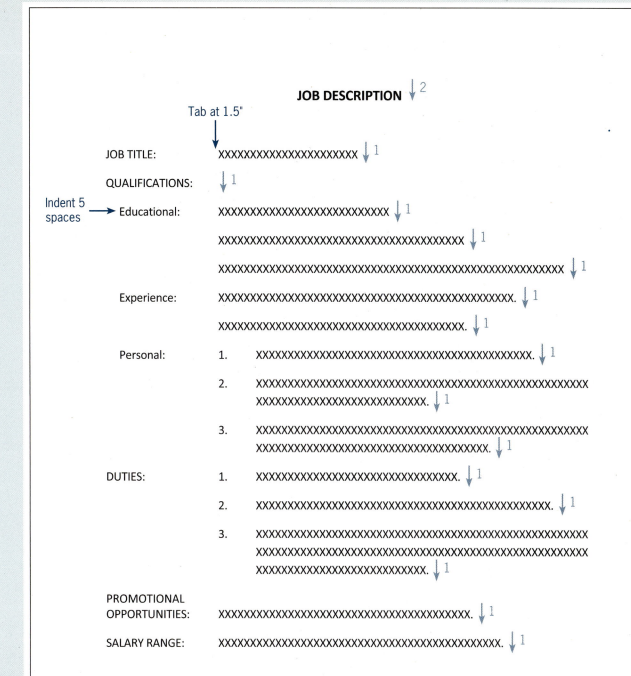

JOB DESCRIPTION ↓ 2

Tab at 1.5"

JOB TITLE: XXXXXXXXXXXXXXXXXXXXX ↓ 1

QUALIFICATIONS: ↓ 1

Indent 5
spaces → Educational: XXXXXXXXXXXXXXXXXXXXXXXXX ↓ 1

XXXXXXXXXXXXXXXXXXXXXXXXXXXXXXXXXX ↓ 1

XXXXXXXXXXXXXXXXXXXXXXXXXXXXXXXXXXXXXXXXXXXXX ↓ 1

Experience: XXXXXXXXXXXXXXXXXXXXXXXXXXXXXXXXXXXXX. ↓ 1

XXXXXXXXXXXXXXXXXXXXXXXXXXXXXX. ↓ 1

Personal: 1.   XXXXXXXXXXXXXXXXXXXXXXXXXXXXXXXXXXXXXX. ↓ 1

2.   XXXXXXXXXXXXXXXXXXXXXXXXXXXXXXXXXXXXXXXXX
XXXXXXXXXXXXXXXXXXXXXXXXX. ↓ 1

3.   XXXXXXXXXXXXXXXXXXXXXXXXXXXXXXXXXXXXXXXXX
XXXXXXXXXXXXXXXXXXXXXXXXXXXXX. ↓ 1

DUTIES: 1.   XXXXXXXXXXXXXXXXXXXXXXXXXXXXXXX. ↓ 1

2.   XXXXXXXXXXXXXXXXXXXXXXXXXXXXXXXXXXXXXXXXX. ↓ 1

3.   XXXXXXXXXXXXXXXXXXXXXXXXXXXXXXXXXXXXXX
XXXXXXXXXXXXXXXXXXXXXXXXXXXXXXXXXXXXXXXXX
XXXXXXXXXXXXXXXXXXXXXXXXXX. ↓ 1

PROMOTIONAL
OPPORTUNITIES: XXXXXXXXXXXXXXXXXXXXXXXXXXXXXXXXXXX. ↓ 1

SALARY RANGE: XXXXXXXXXXXXXXXXXXXXXXXXXXXXXXXXXXXXXX. ↓ 1

OPERATIVE REPORT

NAME: XXXXXXXXXXXXXXXXX   HOSPITAL NUMBER: XXXXXXXXXXXXXX

ADMISSION: XXXXXXXXXXXXXXX   ROOM: XXXXXXXXXXXXX

DISCHARGE: XXXXXXXXXXXXXXXXXXXXX   DICTATED: XXXXXXXXXXXXXXXXX

DATE OF PROCEDURE: XXXXXXXXXXXXXXXXXXXXXXXXX

SURGEON: XXXXXXXXXXXXXXXXXXXXXXXXX

ASSISTANT: XXXXXXXXXXXXXXXXXXXXXXXXXXXXXX

PREOPERATIVE DIAGNOSIS: XXXXXXXXXXXXXXXXXXXXXXXXXXXXXXXXXXXXXXX.

POSTOPERATIVE DIAGNOSIS: XXXXX.

NAME OF OPERATION: XXXXXXXXXXXXXXXXXX.

ANESTHESIA: XXXXXXXXXXXXXXXXXXXXXXXXXXXXXXXXX.

DESCRIPTION OF PROCEDURE: XXXXXXXXXXXXXXXXXXXXXXXXXXXXXXXXXXXXXXXXXXXXXXXXXXXXXXXXX
XXXXXXXXXXXXXXXXXXXXXXXXXXXXXXXXXXXXXXXXXXXXXXXXXXXXXXXXXXXXXXXXXXXXXXXXXXXX
XXXXXXXXXXXXXXXXXXXXXXXXXXXXXXXXXXXXXXXXXXXXXXXXXXXXXXXXXXXXXXXXXXXXXXXXXX
XXXXXXXXXXXXXXXXXXXXXXXXXXXXXXXXXXXXXXXXXXXXXXXXXXXXXXXXXXXXXXXXXXXXXXXXXX
XXXXXXXXXXXXXXXXXXXXXXXXXXXXXXXXXXXXXXXXXXXXXX.

COMPLICATIONS: XXXXX.

ESTIMATED BLOOD LOSS: XXXXXXXXXXXXXXXXX.

REPLACEMENT: XXXXXXXXXXXXXXXXXX.

X-RAYS: XXXXXXXXXXX.

SPECIMEN: XXXXXXXXXXXXX. ↓ 3

_____
XXXXXXXXXXXXXXXXXX (xx) ←— Reference initials
     ↑   ↑
Doctor's name   Two spaces

NOTE: The Operative Report is preprinted with the headings as shown above. Key the information dictated next to the appropriate headings.

1. Transcribe the Word Mastery terms from the Transcription CD.

2. Transcribe the five documents from the Transcription CD following the instructions below and using the current date unless another date is given.

   - Open Document 1 and use plain paper. Key the Job Description for a medical transcriptionist.

   - Open Document 2 and use the Operative Report. Key the information in the appropriate spaces on the form.

   - Open Document 3 and use plain paper. Key the information for the dental report. Use double spacing and the default tab (0.5") for paragraph indents. (*Note:* This report uses double spacing, which is different from the line spacing used in the Unbound Report introduced in Chapter 1. Use the Line Spacing button and select 2.0 before keying this report.)

   - Open Document 4 and use the letterhead for Dental Care Associates. Key the document in block letter style with open punctuation.

   - Open Document 5 and use the letterhead for William A. Noel, D.M.D., PA. Key the document in block letter style with open punctuation.

3. When you have transcribed a document using the file from the Transcription CD, remember to use the **Save As** feature and a distinctive name as the file name for each document.

4. Spell-check, proofread, and submit all five documents to your instructor for approval.

CHAPTER CHECKPOINTS

Place a check mark beside the objectives
you can meet after completing this chapter.

_____ I can define, spell, and use the Word Mastery terms in this chapter.

_____ I can use the commonly misused terms from the Word Usage section in this chapter.

_____ I can spell correctly the words in the Spelling section in this chapter.

_____ I can apply the medical prefixes and suffixes in this chapter.

_____ I can apply the rules from the Language Skills sections in earlier chapters.

_____ I can transcribe a Job Description and proofread carefully.

_____ I can transcribe dental letters and reports, including an Operative Report, and proofread carefully.

Evaluation Form

Access the Evaluation Form from your Transcription CD. Complete it and submit it with your work. You may choose to either print the form and complete it or complete the form electronically.

Chapter 20

ADMISSION LETTER, SURGICAL PATHOLOGY REPORT, DISCHARGE SUMMARY, AND MEDICATION RENEWAL LETTER

As a transcriptionist in a hospital, you will process all of the hospital's correspondence and medical reports. If an error is detected in a document after it has left the transcription department, multiple forms must be completed and distributed, and the amended document must be made available to all doctors concerned. Accuracy and confidentiality are the most important attributes of any successful medical transcriptionist.

LEARNING OBJECTIVES

After completing all the learning activities in this chapter, you will be able to:

- Define, spell, and use the Word Mastery terms.

- Use commonly misused words appropriately.

- Use correct spelling for commonly misspelled words.

- Apply medical prefixes and suffixes presented in this chapter.

- Apply language skills rules presented in earlier chapters.

- Apply proofreading and transcription skills.

- Transcribe medical letters and documents, including a Surgical Pathology Report and a Discharge Summary.

Word Mastery Preview

Directions: Review the list of Word Mastery terms that will be used in the documents you will be transcribing. Learn the definition for each word and how to spell it correctly.

---

omental   *Definition:* pertaining to a fold of the cavity of the abdomen
         Example: The omental region is divided into the greater and lesser omental areas.

---

mesentery   *Definition:* one or more vertebrate membranes that consist of a double fold of the periotoneum and invest the intestines and their appendages
         Example: The elderly lady had several mesentery problems.

---

peritoneal   *Definition:* pertaining to the membrane wall lining the abdominal and pelvic cavities
         Example: Acute and chronic renal failure are among the most common indications for peritoneal dialysis.

---

metastatic   *Definition:*   the transfer of disease from one organ or part to another not directly connected with it
         Example: The cancerous tumors were removed, but there were metastatic possibilities that they could recur.

---

adenocarcinoma *Definition:* cancerous tumor of a gland
         Example: Adenocarcinoma tumor cells form recognizable glandular structures.

---

pancreas   *Definition:* a large, elongated gland located behind the stomach
         Example: The pancreas produces insulin.

---

nodule   *Definition:* a solid node that can be detected by touch
         Example: A surfer's nodule can occur on the bony area of the feet or legs and is the result of kneeling on surfboards.

---

bisected   *Definition:* cut into two parts
         Example: Myrna bisected the tissue for microscopic study.

---

aneurysm   *Definition:* a pouch formed by the localized abnormal relation of the wall on an artery
         Example: The most common site for an arterial aneurysm is the aorta.

| carotid | *Definition:* the principal artery of the neck |
| | *Example:* A pulse may be taken by feeling the carotid artery. |

| angiographies | *Definition:* radiography of vessels of the body |
| | *Example:* The angiographies revealed artery blockage. |

B Word Usage

Directions: Learn to spell and define these confusing words, which may occur within the documents you will be transcribing.

| **discreet** | (adjective) prudent |
| **discrete** | (adjective) distinct or separate |

| **faze** | (verb) to disturb |
| **phase** | (noun) a stage in development |

| **forth** | (adverb) forward or away |
| **fourth** | (adjective) next after third |

| **may be** | (verb) a verb consisting of two words |
| **maybe** | (adverb) perhaps |

| **reality** | (noun) realism or certainty |
| **realty** | (noun) real estate |

| **tale** | (noun) fable or falsehood |
| **tell** | (verb) inform |

were	(verb) form of the verb *to be*
we're	(pronoun and verb) contraction of *we are*
where	(adverb) at, in, or what place

C Spelling

Directions: Learn to spell these common words.

analysis	incidentally	psychology
cemetery	pamphlet	referral
enthusiasm	peculiar	rhythm
grammar	personally	sergeant
height	professor	warranty

D Language Skills

Directions: Knowing various prefixes and suffixes used within the medical fields will help you become more familiar with the meanings of medical terms. Some of these prefixes and suffixes are used in the Word Mastery terms you are studying within the chapter. Learn each prefix or suffix and its meaning.

Prefix or Suffix	Meaning
angio-	vessel
dys-	bad, painful, difficult
hystero-	uterus, womb
-megaly	enlargement
meta-	beyond, change
-ostomy	new opening
patho-	disease
-phobia	fear
-stenosis	narrowing, stricture
-tomy	incision

ENGLISH SKILLS EXERCISES

A Word Mastery

Directions: Apply what you learned in the English Skills Review. Choose the correct word in the following sentences from those found in the Word Mastery Preview.

1. The doctors said her cancer was _____ because it had spread to other parts of her body.

2. Although we can live without our spleen, we cannot live without our _____.

3. In many biology classes, students _____ tissues from frogs.

4. A(n) _____ can occur in the heart or in the brain.

5. Her physician wanted to take _____ to determine if she had blockage in her arteries.

6. _____ dialysis may be required with chronic renal failure.

7. Abigail had a cancerous tumor of the gland, which is called a(n)

   _____.

8. John felt his _____ artery to see how fast his pulse was after he exercised.

9. A(n) _____ had formed on one of his knees from kneeling to pray daily.

10. The surgeon wanted to examine the _____ area in his abdomen.

B Word Usage

Directions: Choose the correct word in each of the following sentences.

1. She was (forth, fourth) in her class when she completed medical school.

2. What (faze, phase) in life do you think most people enjoy the most?

3. Medical personnel must be very (discreet, discrete) with the information they collect from patients.

4. Many children love their parents to (tale, tell) them bedtime stories.

5. You (may be, maybe) interested in becoming a physician one day.

6. (We're, Were, Where) do you think you will want to work when you graduate?

7. (May be, Maybe) our instructor will let us know our final grade on the project soon.

8. There are many (reality, realty) shows on television, but I prefer to watch sporting events.

9. Do you think (we're, were, where) going to be working on the research grant together?

10. As you (we're, were, where) coming into the office, the receptionist was calling you to remind you of your appointment.

C Spelling

Directions: Choose the correct spelling in each of the following sentences.

1. I was so impressed by the (height, heigth) of the police (sargent, sergeant).

2. The (proffessor, professor) of human (psychology, pyschology) said he would be grading our research on content, punctuation, and (grammar, grammer).

3. Because we wanted to select a burial plot in the nearby (cemetary, cemetery), my husband picked up a (pamphlet, pamplet) from Woodland Funeral Home for us to review.

4. (Incidentally, Incidentaly), you will be happy to know that I (personally, personaly) asked the chef to prepare your favorite dish.

Spelling (continued)

5. After much time and a great deal of (analyses, analysis), we decided it was best to postpone the project until more funding could be secured.

6. She demonstrated so much (enthuseasm, enthusiasm) for the position that the sales director hired her immediately.

7. Some people seem to have no (rhythm, rythm), and they look awkward when they try to dance.

8. Be sure to ask a person for his/her permission if you plan to use him/her as a (referal, referral) during a job interview.

9. When I purchased my car, there was no (warrantee, warranty) because it was a used vehicle.

10. I found it very (pecular, peculiar) that no one was in the waiting room ahead of me.

D Language Skills

Directions: Use proofreaders' marks to make corrections in the following sentences. Write "Correct" by the sentence if no corrections are needed. Some of these sentences include a review of language skills presented in previous chapters. You may want to refer to the reference manual in the back of this text-workbook for a review before completing these examples.

1. Toby Pennell dean of the medical college was to speak at the commencement exercises.

2. The *Journal Of The American Association For Medical Transcription* is an excellent bimonthly journal.

3. You will need to complete the following steps 1. Read the information in your chapter. 2. Study the word mastery terms, medical prefixes and medical suffixes. 3. Review the rules in the language skills section from previous chapters.

4. Your application for graduation will amount to twenty-five dollars ($25).

5. The test will cover chapters two and three.

6. The Journal of the American Association for Medical Transcription is a publication many medical transcriptionists read.

7. Be sure to read all the material and complete all the work in Chapters Seventeen to Twenty before you take your next test.

8. Here is the procedure to follow before you go to Part 4: (1) Complete the Proofreading test, (2) Take the written test, and (3) Take the transcription test.

9. If you study you will do well on your test however if you do not study you will probably not score as well.

10. All the material in this text-workbook has been designed to help you be successful in transcribing proofreading and correcting documents.

Fill in the prefixes or suffixes for the meanings listed below:

incision   _____

fear   _____

enlargement   _____

uterus, womb   _____

disease   _____

E Composition

1. Compose and key a paragraph applying the word mastery, word usage, spelling, and language skills you have studied.

2. Compose and key a second paragraph that describes some of the Health Insurance Portability and Accountability Act (HIPAA) regulations that help ensure the confidentiality of patients. You may find it helpful to conduct research online or at a medical facility.

3. Compose and key a third paragraph that explains the importance of accuracy in medical records. Submit all three paragraphs to your instructor.

F Research

1. Locate five recent articles from newspapers, magazines, the library, or the Internet that relate to medical ethics, medical cases, medical documents, medical terminology, or the medical profession that you did not use in previous chapters.

2. List the source and date of each article and summarize it in paragraph format. Include your name and the date. Proofread, edit, and revise the paragraphs to correct all grammar and spelling errors. Print the documents. Proofread them again and make any final changes before submitting them to your instructor.

TRANSCRIPTION PREVIEW

In this chapter you will key five documents using letterheads and two forms. The two forms—the Surgical Pathology Report and the Discharge Summary—are preprinted. You will listen to the dictation and key the information in the forms. Review the examples that follow to become familiar with the Surgical Pathology Report and the Discharge Summary.

SURGICAL PATHOLOGY REPORT

PATIENT: XXXXX   ACCESS NO.:   XXXX

ADDRESS: XXXXXXXXX   HOSPITAL NO.:   XXXX
XXXXXXXXXXXXXXXXX

AGE/SEX: XX/X   CPT CODE: XXXXXXXXXXXX

SOCIAL SECURITY NO.: XXXXXXXXXX

SURGEON: XXXXXXXXXXXX   DATE OF OPERATION: XXXXXXXXXXXX

RESIDENT: XXXXXXXXX   DATE OF REPORT: XXXXXXXXXXXX

ATTENDING PHYSICIAN: XXXXXXXXXXXX

COPY TO PHYSICIAN: XXXXXXXXXXXX

PRE OP DX: XXXXXXXXXX

OPERATION: XXXXXXXXXX

POST OP DX: XXXXXXXXXX

TISSUES REMOVED: A.   XXXXXXXXXXXX ↓1

Indent 1.5" ⟶ B.   XXXXXXXXXXXXXX ↓1

                   C.   XXXXXXXXXXXXXXXXXXX ↓3

OR CONSULT: XXXXXXXXXXXXXXXXXXXXXXXXXXXXXXXXXXXXXXXXXXXXXX ↓2

INTRA/EXTRA CONSULT: XXXXXXXXXX

===

Page 1 of 2

(Continued)

NOTE: The Surgical Pathology Report is preprinted with the headings as shown above. Key the information dictated next to the appropriate headings. Additional text will be dictated and should be formatted as shown above and on the next page.

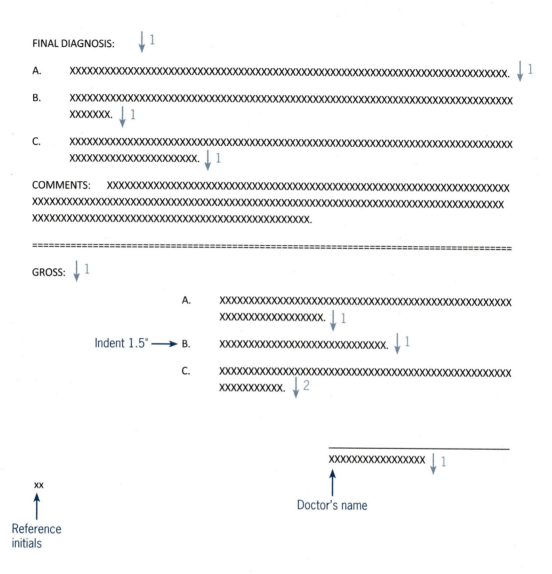

FINAL DIAGNOSIS: ↓1

A.   XXXXXXXXXXXXXXXXXXXXXXXXXXXXXXXXXXXXXXXXXXXXXXXXXXXXXXXXXXXXXXXXXXXXXXX. ↓1

B.   XXXXXXXXXXXXXXXXXXXXXXXXXXXXXXXXXXXXXXXXXXXXXXXXXXXXXXXXXXXXXXXXXXXXX
XXXXXXX. ↓1

C.   XXXXXXXXXXXXXXXXXXXXXXXXXXXXXXXXXXXXXXXXXXXXXXXXXXXXXXXXXXXXXXXXXXXXX
XXXXXXXXXXXXXXXXXXXXXXXXXXX. ↓1

COMMENTS: XXXXXXXXXXXXXXXXXXXXXXXXXXXXXXXXXXXXXXXXXXXXXXXXXXXXXXXXXXXXXXXX
XXXXXXXXXXXXXXXXXXXXXXXXXXXXXXXXXXXXXXXXXXXXXXXXXXXXXXXXXXXXXXXXXXXXXXXXXXXXXXXXXXXX
XXXXXXXXXXXXXXXXXXXXXXXXXXXXXXXXXXXXXXXXXXXXXXXXXX.

==

GROSS: ↓1

        A.   XXXXXXXXXXXXXXXXXXXXXXXXXXXXXXXXXXXXXXXXXXXXXXX
XXXXXXXXXXXXXXXXXX. ↓1

Indent 1.5" ⟶ B.   XXXXXXXXXXXXXXXXXXXXXXXXXXXXXXX. ↓1

        C.   XXXXXXXXXXXXXXXXXXXXXXXXXXXXXXXXXXXXXXXXXXXXXXX
XXXXXXXXXXX. ↓2

_____
XXXXXXXXXXXXXXXX ↓1

Doctor's name

XX

Reference
initials

Page 2 of 2

DISCHARGE SUMMARY

PATIENT NAME: XXXXXXXXXXXXXX

PATIENT NUMBER: XXXXXXXXX

ADMISSION DATE: XXXXXXXXXXX

DISCHARGE DATE: XXXXXXXXXXX

**ATTENDING
PHYSICIAN:**   XXXXXXXXXXXXXXXXXXXX ↓ 1

XXXXXXXXXXXXXXXXXXXXXXXXXXXXXXXXXXXXXXXXXXXXXXXXXXXXXXXXXXXXXXXX
XXXXXXXXXXXXXXXXXXXXXXXXXXXXXXXXXXXXXXXXXXXXXXXXXXXXXXXXXXXXXXXX
XXXXXXXXXXXXXXXXXXXXXXXXXXXXXXXXXXXXXXXXXXXXXXXXXXXXXXXXXXXXXXXX
XXXXXXXXXXXXXXXXXXXXXXXXXXXXXXXXXXXX. ↓ 1

FINAL DIAGNOSIS: 1. XXXXXXXXXXXXXXXXXXXXXXXXXXXXXX. ↓ 1

Indent 1.5" → 2. XXXXXXXXXXXXXXXXXXXXXXXXXXXXX. ↓ 3

Signed_____

XXXXXXXXXXXXXXXXXXXXXX ↓ 1

↑
Doctor's
name

XX/xx

↑
Reference
initials

NOTE: The Discharge Summary is preprinted with the headings as shown above. Key the information dictated next to the appropriate headings. Additional text will be dictated and should be formatted as shown above.

1. Transcribe the Word Mastery terms from the Transcription CD.

2. Transcribe the five documents from the Transcription CD following the instructions below and using the current date unless another date is given.

   - Open Document 1 and use the letterhead for Good Fellowship Community Hospital. Key the document in block letter style with mixed punctuation.

   - Open Document 2 and use the Surgical Pathology Report. Key the information in the appropriate spaces.

   - Open Document 3 and use the Discharge Summary form. Key the information in the appropriate spaces.

   - Open Document 4 and use the Discharge Summary form. Key the information in the appropriate spaces.

   - Open Document 5 and use the letterhead for Superior Pharmaceuticals Manager. Key the document in block letter style with mixed punctuation.

3. When you have transcribed a document using the file from the Transcription CD, remember to use the **Save As** feature and a distinctive name as the file name for each document.

4. Spell-check, proofread, and submit all five documents to your instructor for approval.

CHAPTER CHECKPOINTS

Place a check mark beside the objectives
you can meet after completing this chapter.

_____ I can define, spell, and use the Word Mastery terms in this chapter.

_____ I can use the commonly misused terms from the Word Usage section
in this chapter.

_____ I can spell correctly the words in the Spelling section in this chapter.

_____ I can apply the medical prefixes and suffixes in this chapter.

_____ I can apply the rules from the Language Skills sections in earlier chapters.

_____ I can transcribe medical letters and documents, including a Surgical
Pathology Report and a Discharge Summary, and proofread carefully.

Evaluation Form

Access the Evaluation Form from your Transcription CD. Complete it and
submit it with your work. You may choose to either print the form and
complete it or complete the form electronically.

**IMPORTANT NOTE: Check with your instructor regarding
the testing procedures for Part 3 (Chapters 13–20).**

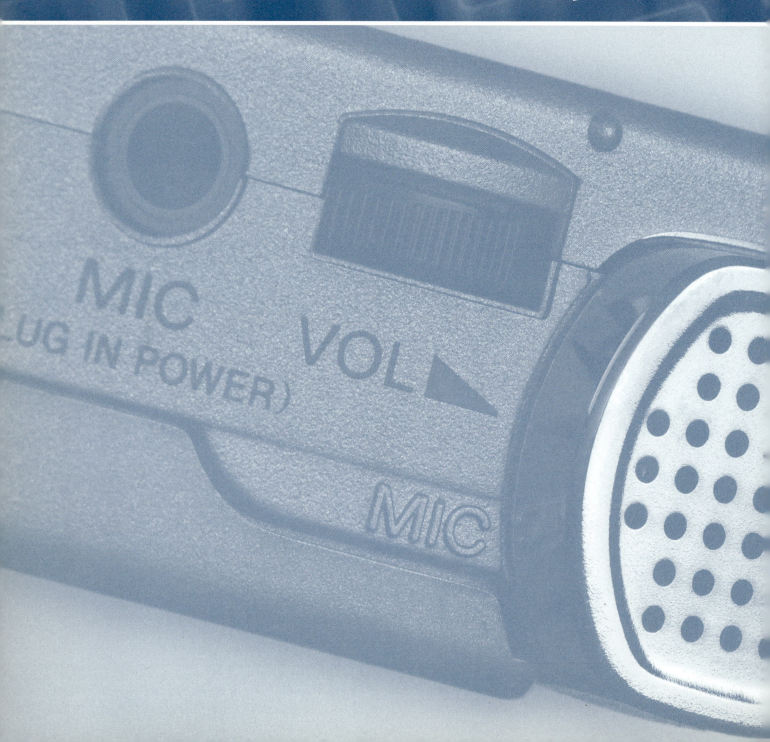

PART 4
Dictation and Continuous Speech Recognition

Jean Sutton, Columbia, SC
Medical Transcriptionist, Dorn Veterans Administration Hospital

Why did you decide to do this type of work?

"I decided to do this type of work because I thought it would be something I would enjoy. I felt that it would be relatively easy to find a job in this field. As a blind person, I felt that this would be a job where I could work independently. With the advent of personal computers and speech software, I felt even more comfortable with my ability to do the job well. Also, this job fit my personality. I enjoy sitting and typing all day."

The thing I enjoy most about transcribing is learning new things and being able to work independently.

Who inspired you to consider working in transcription?

"At the school for the blind I attended, I took keyboarding courses for several years, beginning in the sixth grade. This is when I first thought of using this skill in a job. Then I became pen pals with a woman who was a medical transcriptionist, and her job sounded interesting. She was also blind."

Where did you learn how to transcribe?

"I graduated from the University of South Carolina with a degree in psychology and was accepted in the Masters Social Work program. But after only two days, I decided that wasn't really what I wanted to do, so I went to Midlands Technical College and got a certificate in medical transcription. My courses at Midlands Tech included anatomy classes and medical terminology classes."

When did you first begin transcribing?

"Shortly after graduating from Midlands Technical College, I got a job at the VA Hospital."

What do you enjoy the most and the least about transcribing?

"What I enjoy the most about transcribing is learning new things all the time and being able to work independently. What I like least about medical transcription is the pay. I feel that my pay should better reflect the knowledge and skill needed in this occupation."

What advice would you give a student regarding transcription?

"Transcription has changed so much in 28 years. I would advise those interested in this field to make sure that this type of work fits their personality. If you like a lot of interaction with other people, this might not be the job for you. You should have a good knowledge of grammar and spelling, be able to understand foreign dictators with accents, and have good listening skills."

© Andy Dean Photography/Shutterstock.com

In the previous chapters, you have had the experience of transcribing dictation. Part 4 will give you the hands-on experience of dictating information. Many business people do not use dictating as a means of input because they have never been trained and do not feel confident in using the equipment.

You also will learn about continuous speech recognition technology. This technology uses the voice and a computer to convert spoken words to text. Although you will be given information about dictating and continuous speech recognition, you will not actually have hands-on experience using this technology unless you have access to the equipment. Your instructor will advise you.

DICTATION GUIDELINES

The quality and accuracy of the transcription process often depends on the skills of the dictator. To help produce a good recording, follow the guidelines below.

1. Have all references or resource materials to which you might need to refer nearby.

2. Organize your thoughts by using an outline or brief notes of the material you wish to dictate.

3. Identify whether the dictation is a draft or final copy.

4. Discuss the format that is to be used, such as unbound report format or block letter style with open punctuation.

5. Indicate if the document will need enclosures or copies.

6. Pronounce each word clearly and spell any word that has an unusual spelling or that could be confused with another word.

   Example: Jean or Jon for John.

   Some letters sound alike; therefore, it might be helpful to give examples to ensure the transcriptionist understands.

   Example: Send the letter to P. T. Brown. Transcriptionist, that is "P" as in Peter and "T" as in Tom.

7. Use the expressions listed below to indicate the correct type of capitalization to use with the dictation:

   "Capital" means capitalize only the first letter of the next word.

   Example: (Capital) Columbia.

   "Caps" means capitalize the first letter of each major word in the following group of related words.

   Example: At our meeting, I will make the (Caps) Time Management speech to the (Caps) Fashion Institute.

   "All Caps" means use all capital letters in the next group of words until the originator says "End all caps."

   Example: This presentation is based on your (All Caps) TIMESAVER (End All Caps) calendar.

8. Dictate any punctuation or paragraph notations that might be helpful to the transcriptionist.

9. Indicate when a document is needed and whether it is a top priority document that needs to be transcribed quickly.

10. Be sure to state your name if the transcriptionist transcribes documents for many originators so she or he will know to whom to return the transcribed materials.

DICTATION AND TRANSCRIPTION PROCEDURES

1. Your instructor will give you information regarding the software and equipment you need to use to record and transcribe your dictation. Two sources that are simple to use are Express Dictate and Express Scribe, which can be downloaded from the Internet. Instructions for using these programs are given below. You will also need a microphone that is compatible with your computer.

2. Before you begin, complete these steps:

   • Have the information you want to dictate accessible.

   • Review the dictation guidelines on the previous page.

3. Once you are ready to dictate using Express Dictate, follow these steps:

   • Plug your microphone into the correct receptacle in your computer.

   • Click on Express Dictate (which should have already been downloaded to your computer).

   • Click on Dictation.

   • Click on New.

   • Click on the record button (red dot icon on screen).

   • Dictate the information you want to record.

   • Click the stop button (small square icon on screen).

   • Click on Dictation to continue to dictate.

   • After you have finished your dictation, save it as a .dct file.

4. Once you are ready to transcribe using Express Scribe, follow these steps:

   • Remove the microphone and plug in your headset into the correct receptacle in your computer.

   • Click on Express Scribe.

   • Click on File.

   • Click on Load Dictation File.

   • Click on the file that contains your recorded dictation (look for the .dct file).

   • Click play and begin transcribing.

DICTATION AND TRANSCRIPTION EXERCISES

Review the language skills presented in previous chapters as well as the format for unbound reports. You can refer to the reference manual in the back of this text-workbook. Read the preceding information about dictation guidelines and dictation and transcription procedures. Then complete the following exercises.

Exercise 1: Dictate the two introductory paragraphs that appear on page 222. Use the title "Dictation and Continuous Speech Recognition."

Exercise 2: Dictate the information about continuous speech recognition that follows. Note that the information does not include punctuation and paragraphing. You will have to supply these as you dictate. You will see how valuable the language skills you learned in previous chapters will be in completing this activity.

Continuous Speech Recognition

Continuous speech recognition is an interesting concept that uses the human voice as an input device to the computer. If you want to use this concept you must have the proper software such as Dragon NaturallySpeaking L&H Voice Xpress or IBM ViaVoice. There are certain hardware and software requirements and you must enroll and train the software so it can adjust to your voice patterns. You will have to learn how to control the microphone dictate the text enter punctuation marks create breaks and delete errors. In addition to this training you also need to learn how to change and correct text create special characters and numbers make document changes and format text.

Exercise 3: Read the information titled "Speech Technology Basics" beginning on page 226. Then research additional information on continuous speech recognition by using the Internet or library or by contacting office technology and/or equipment suppliers. Compose a one-page report about continuous speech recognition based on your research. The experience you gained in completing the composition and research sections in the previous chapters will be valuable to you as you complete this activity. Dictate the one-page report you compiled.

Exercise 4: Eventually the goal in dictating is to be able to do so with very few notes. If you write something out completely before dictating, it would have been just as easy to key the document yourself rather than gettting someone else to transcribe it for you, assuming you have keyboarding skills, English skills, and knowledge of proper formatting. To practice dictating information without the aid of written notes, dictate the following six items that relate to you and this course:

- your name
- your instructor's name
- the name of your training institution
- the name of the course for which you are completing this activity
- a short description of what you have enjoyed the most about the course
- a short description of how you have benefited from taking this course

Exercise 5: Transcribe the four exercises that you dictated into four unbound reports. Add an appropriate title to each report if a title is not dictated. Spell-check, proofread, and submit the four documents to your instructor for approval. Your instructor may also ask you to submit your dictation files.

Additional Exercises: If you have access to some type of continuous speech recognition software, such as Dragon NaturallySpeaking, your instructor may provide additional exercises to give you hands-on experience using this technology.

SPEECH TECHNOLOGY BASICS

Continuous speech recognition (CSR) uses the voice as a computer input device. The computer then converts the spoken words to text. After decades of speculation about when speech recognition would be ready for prime time, CSR programs are now gaining popularity. With increased processor speeds, declining memory costs, and increased storage capacity, the modern computer can be a talking-typing machine.

You may already be familiar with some type of speech recognition that is not limited to a single speaker. Speech recognition includes voice user interfaces. If you have speak-text applications on your cellular phone, you can speak, and the information appears as a text message. If you have made calls to a call center, they may have been answered by a recording that asks for input from you. You speak and the "simulated person" (recording) on the other end "listens" to what you have said and "responds." Sometimes the communication goes well; sometimes it does not. Thus, you can see some of the challenges of speech recognition.

The voice revolution began in the 1960s at IBM's famed Thomas J. Watson Research Center in Hawthorne, New York. IBM has long believed that the next jump in computer productivity would be caused by a voice-interface revolution. To this end, it committed three decades of research to study voice recognition. And IBM was not alone in its belief in the potential of voice-typing. While IBM was introducing its CSR software called *ViaVoice,* other companies were introducing CSR systems of their own.

- Dragon Systems impressed customers and analysts alike with *NaturallySpeaking.*
- Lernout & Hauspie excited the crowd with *Voice Xpress.*
- Philips shined the spotlight on its *FreeSpeech* software.
- Dozens of smaller companies began to compete in the vigorous CSR marketplace.

The speech recognition software now available has progressed to the point that, when you talk, your computer can type your words accurately.

The Dream Versus the Reality

After the basics have been conquered, it takes additional time of dedicated practice to train your computer to understand your unique way of speaking. However, if you work at it, the results can be astounding. A typical person who spends adequate time training the software can expect to voice-type between 110 and 160 words per minute (wpm) with 90 to 98 percent accuracy.

Health and Safety Issues

Beyond the obvious input efficiencies for data entry, there are other reasons why businesses and schools are accepting voice. In February 1999, the Occupational Safety and Health Administration (OSHA) released a draft proposal on how employers must reduce repetitive strain injuries (RSI) and carpal tunnel syndrome in the workplace. OSHA calls these injuries *work-related musculoskeletal disorders* or WMSDs.

Speech represents a very important weapon in the battle against WMSDs. It is interesting to note that the sharp rise in WMSDs corresponds with the infusion of personal computers into the workplace starting in the mid 1980s. While most WMSDs still occur in the manufacturing sector, office workers who use a computer keyboard and a mouse now account for a significantly high portion of WMSDs.

Speech dictation can help office workers who depend on keyboarding for their livelihoods. CSR systems can dramatically reduce the number of repetitive keystrokes these workers must make each day. Does this mean that some office workers can quit typing and use voice instead? For many suffering with WMSDs, the answer is an empathetic YES! For many carpal tunnel syndrome and RSI sufferers, a voice is a highly effective alternative to keyboarding.

Blending Keyboarding with Voice Input

Most of us will continue to key documents. It is, therefore, essential that keyboarding instructors continue to emphasize correct keying techniques and proper computer-office ergonomics.

In some situations it will be difficult, if not impossible, to use a CSR program; for instance, taking notes on your computer during a lecture or during a sales conference. Also, speaking all day to a computer can cause problems with your vocal cords. If you are going to use voice dictation software, you had better keep your water bottle handy and give your voice a rest by keying with your hands every once in a while!

However, if you use a CSR program for even 50 percent of the time you spend in front of a computer, your chances of suffering severe WMSDs as you get older will diminish. So, if for no other reason than to avoid future long-term pain and suffering, a CSR program is well worth investigating.

Hardware and Software Requirements

With CSR systems, the faster your CPU and the greater your computer's memory capacity the better. Be sure to check your CSR software for exact specifications required.

CSR Training

CSR software training can be divided into four parts:

- enrollment and initial training
- training yourself in the basics
- training your computer to understand your distinctive voice
- practicing

All of this can take several hours to complete.

Enrollment and Initial Training

Obviously, before you can do anything you must install your software, register yourself as a user, and make sure your microphone headset is working properly. Then you must proceed through a required initial training that will teach your computer to understand your unique accent and way of speaking.

Installation and Headset Adjustment

The installation process is very straightforward. Read each screen and follow the instructions your software provides. You will be asked to enter your name, and then, with your headset on, your CSR program will walk you through several steps to make sure your headset is connected properly. The software will then adjust its audio settings to the volume of your voice.

Microphone Position

CSR software works best when your headset is one-half to one inch away from your mouth and the tip of the microphone is placed slightly below your lower lip. It may also help to place the microphone slightly to one side of your mouth. You will need to experiment to find the best position. Once you find that position, be consistent! Place the microphone in the same position every time you use your CSR software.

If your microphone is too far away from your mouth, your recognition accuracy will be poor. If your microphone is too close to your mouth and nose, breathing errors will occur. A breathing error is caused by your breath brushing across the microphone and results in words like "the," "and," and "but" being printed across the screen.

Training Your Software

Once your headset is working properly, you will be asked to read a series of sentences. The idea behind this training process is to record enough samples of your speech so the software can adjust to your voice patterns.

With most CSR programs, you will be recording sentences for 20 to 60 minutes. Don't despair. This is an important step that cannot be avoided. Do not skip this step if you ever hope to achieve any level of accuracy. Give your computer a chance to understand you!

Once you have trained your software, you need to learn the commands that will allow you to format and punctuate your document. These commands are similar to the commands that a person uses in dictating a document to be transcribed. The commands tell the software such things as where to place punctuation and when to begin a new paragraph. Each CSR program has its own set of commands. Some of the programs also have *natural language commands* that allow you to give the same command in several different ways.

Just as you have learned that practice is required to develop good transcription skills, you will find that practice is required to develop the skills needed to use voice recognition software effectively.

CHECKPOINTS

Place a check mark beside the objectives
you can meet after completing Part 4.

_____ I can operate the dictating features of my recording software and
equipment properly.

_____ I can use my researching, writing, and communication skills correctly.

_____ I can organize my thoughts and dictate correspondence using the recording
software and equipment.

_____ I can transcribe documents in unbound report format.

_____ I understand the basics of continuous speech recognition.

Evaluation Form

Access the Part 4 Evaluation Form from your Transcription CD. Complete it
and submit it with your work. You may choose to either print the form and
complete it or complete the form electronically.

REFERENCE MANUAL

PROOFREADING GUIDELINES

Proofreaders' Marks

Symbol	Meaning	Example	After Revising
∧	insert text	*Traffic* Winn∧Engineering	Winn Traffic Engineering
∧	insert comma	Cincinnati∧Ohio	Cincinnati, Ohio
∨	insert apostrophe	Whitney∨s computer	Whitney's computer
⌶	insert hyphen	first⌶class service	first-class service
⊙	insert period	Meet me there⊙	Meet me there.
⌒	close up	can⌒not	cannot
#	insert space	take#time	take time
tr or ∩	transpose	retreive	retrieve
/c	lowercase	/c /c QUALITY CONTROL	quality control
⟋	delete	posstal	postal
/	replace	7 a.m.	7 p.m.
————	underline	<u>Media Mess</u>	<u>Media</u> <u>Mess</u>
≡ or cap	capitalize	transcription skills	Transcription Skills
sp	spell out	sp ⑥-day vacation	six-day vacation
¶	new paragraph	...complete.¶Your work was excellent.	...complete. Your work was excellent.
... or stet	let stand; ignore the correction	*stet* just ~~in case~~	just in case
⊐	move right	<u>Plea</u>se call before leaving the office.	Please call before leaving the office.
⊏	move left	Please call before leaving the office.	Please call before leaving the office.
♂	move copy as indicated	Madison's City⌐ ⟨Budget⟩	Madison's City Budget

Proofreading Tips

- When proofreading any document, assume there are errors and look for them as though you were the instructor grading your assignment.
- Do not rely on spelling and grammar features in software programs to correct all errors. Certain types of errors are not recognized by the software.
- Mark corrections using proofreaders' marks, which are shown on the previous page.
- Allow yourself enough time to proofread all documents. Time restraints and deadlines in business may cause you to rush this step. However, you need to be sure to make the time to look over each document carefully.
- Make sure you proofread when you are most alert. This usually means that proofreading at the very beginning of your day or at the end of the day is not the most effective time to do so.
- Don't proofread a document immediately after you have keyed it. Take time to do another task before proofreading the document. By doing so, you won't be relying on what you think you keyed, and you will be more focused on what you really see.
- Proofread your document once for appearance and proper formatting.
- Proofread your document a second time to see if the message has been conveyed correctly and is easy to understand. Will the reader know what is expected of him or her?
- Proofread your document a third time for grammar, punctuation, and spelling errors. The spell-check and grammar-check features of your word processor may not find all your errors for you.
- Although the person for whom you are keying a document is repsonsible for the content, it is important that you check mathematical calculations for accuracy. The person who dictated the document could have made an error. Is there a mathematical error made in the example below?

  We would like to order five black office chairs, Item # 3568, at $150 each (which includes tax). You will find our check for $600 enclosed in our letter.

  (Yes, there is an error: 5 × $150 = $750, not $600 as keyed.)

- Check to be sure that rows of numbers are aligned horizontally and that figures within a column are aligned vertically at the decimal point. Make sure no numbers have been deleted or moved.
- If you are keying a column of numbers from an original copy of a document or dictated document, add the numbers from the original copy or the dictated information to get a total; then add the numbers of what you have just keyed to get a total. The totals should equal. If they do not and the difference between the totals can be divided by nine, you have transposed a number. See the example that follows.

Original Copy	Keyed Copy
10 boxes	*10 boxes*
5 tables	*5 tables*
12 chairs	*21 chairs*

The total of the items in the original copy is 27; the total of the items in the keyed copy is 36. The difference between the two is 9 which can be divided by 9. You will note that *21 chairs* in the keyed copy should have been *12 chairs*.

- When proofreading material, check your punctuation marks very carefully. You would be surprised how much difference punctuation can make in the meaning of a sentence. Look at the examples below:

  The business owner stated, "The customer is always right."

  "The business owner," stated the customer, "is always right."

  Note in the two examples above that both sentences include the exact same words; however, the way each sentence has been punctuated makes a major difference. In the first example, the business owner is speaking and states that the customer is always right. In the second example, the customer is speaking and states that the business owner is always right.

- Check your facts correctly. Don't assume that the originator who dictated the information or the writer who wrote the information has listed all the information correctly. Can you find the errors in the following paragraph?

  I have visited one state capital every year for the past five years. The state capitals I have visited are Atlanta, Georgia; Charleston, South Carolina; Charlotte, North Carolina; and Tallahassee, Florida.

  There are several errors. Charleston and Charlotte are not the capitals of the states mentioned. Columbia is the state capital of South Carolina, and Raleigh is the state capital of North Carolina. The originator stated he/she had visited a state capital every year for the past five years; however, only four cities, not five, are mentioned.

- Keep several reference materials nearby when you proofread. Some suggestions of materials that will be helpful to you are as follows: (1) a dictionary, (2) a thesaurus, and (3) a reference manual. Be sure you are using the most recent editions for any reference material.

- A dictionary can help you determine the correct spelling, pronunciation, and definition of a word.

- A thesaurus can give you synonyms and antonyms for various words.

- Reference manuals contain an assortment of information. Grammar rules about commas, semicolons, hyphens, dashes, colons, capitalization, number/figure style, abbreviation, and word division are included. Format styles and guidelines are also included in reference manuals. Proper forms of address are also incorporated.

- If you give a reference location in a document, make sure the reference is in the location to which you refer the reader.

- If someone receives a letter in which his or her name is misspelled or the wrong name is used, he or she may form a bad impression of the person or business that sent the letter.

- Be sure to check all letter addresses carefully when you proofread. Be sure the correct courtesy title (Miss, Mr., Mrs., Ms., Dr., etc.) is used, the name is correct and correctly spelled, and the letter address and ZIP code are correct. In addition, make sure the correct name is used in the salutation within the correspondence.
- As you proofread any document you have keyed, be sure parallel ideas are expressed in parallel form. For example, adjectives should be paralleled by adjectives, nouns by nouns, infinitives by infinitives, etc. What is wrong in the following example?

    Rachel likes to file papers, answering the phone, and keying documents.

    To *file* is an infinitive (to + a verb); *answering* and *keying* are gerunds (form of a verb that ends in "ing"). Both of the following sentences use parallel structure, and either is acceptable.

    Rachel likes to file papers, to answer the phone, and to key documents.

    Rachel likes filing papers, answering the phone, and keying documents.

- Check the ending of lines and the beginning of lines to make sure there are no duplications or omissions. What is wrong in the lines below?

    I asked my clients to give me all the information they had regarding the case
    case because I could not represent them if they were not totally open and
    and honest with me.

    Notice that the word *case* and the word *and* ended lines and also began the next lines. Unfortunately, when we see the end of a line or end of a page, it causes us to lose our concentration and become careless in proofreading.
- Check the ending of a page and the beginning of the next page to make sure there are no duplications or omissions.
- Check to be sure all pages of your document are in the correct order and no page is missing.
- Check to be sure any enclosure or attachment mentioned in your document is enclosed or attached.
- If you key a list or steps that one should take to accomplish a task or procedure, ask someone who is not familiar with the task or procedure to read what you have keyed and see if she or he would be able to perform the task or procedure based on the list or steps stated.
- If you key directions to a location, ask someone who is not familiar with that location to read what you have keyed to see if he or she would be able to find the location based on the directions stated. In the example given below, is the individual to turn right or to turn left at the intersection?

    When you come to the intersection of Main Street and Elm Street, turn and my office will be two blocks on your left.

- When proofreading a document on your computer screen, focus on viewing just a line at a time and use the downward directional arrow to access each successive line.
- If you are proofreading a printed document, focus on viewing just a line at a time by using some type of device (another sheet of paper or a ruler) to keep your eye focused on one line at a time.

- Use the *Print Preview* feature of Microsoft Word to review a document prior to printing. In this layout, you can view a reduced size of your document on the computer screen. By viewing the document at one glance, you can check the format, alignment, etc.
- By using the *Print Preview* feature, you can reduce excessive printing and wastage of paper. Using less paper saves money, trees, and landfill space.
- Take advantage of the spelling and grammar check tool in your word processing program. It will flag misspelled words and grammatical errors as well as provide suggestions on how to correct them.
- Although some errors will be detected, do not rely totally on the spelling and grammar check tool to find all of the errors. For example, find the five errors that the spelling and grammar check tool did not find in the sentence below.

  When you leaf the doctors office be sure to take your peals when you get to you're home.

  The correct version of the sentence is as follows. (The undetected errors are shown in bold.)

  *When you **leave** the **doctor's** office**,** be sure to take your **pills** when you get to **your** home.*

- Proper lighting is essential while proofreading.
- Reading a document aloud keeps you more focused on it as you proofread.
- Finding ways to relieve stress, such as listening to music or chewing gum, helps you relax as you proofread.
- Although you may be proficient in proofreading, there are probably certain types of errors that you consistently overlook, such as formatting, spelling, grammar, or punctuation errors. Keep a checklist to help you look specifically for those types of errors.
- Remember, the shortest pencil (or in this case, a keyed or written list) is better than the longest memory.

Frequently Misspelled Words

absence	advantageous	athlete
acceptable	advertisement	average
accidentally	advisable	balance
accommodate	aggression	basically
accounting	allege	before
accumulate	allegiance	beginning
achievement	almost	believe
acknowledgment	amateur	beneficial
acquaintance	amend	benefited
acquire	among	breathe
acquisition	analysis	brilliant
acquit	annually	burglar
acreage	apparent	business
across	appreciate	calendar
address	argument	campaign